samurai sketches

From the Bloody Final Years of the Shogun

ALSO BY ROMULUS HILLSBOROUGH

RYOMA – Life of a Renaissance Samurai

SAMURAI
SKETCHES

From the Bloody Final Years of the Shogun

ROMULUS   HILLSBOROUGH

RIDGEBACK
PRESS

San Francisco

Book design by Hiromi Yoshikawa

For information contact:
Ridgeback Press
151 Valdez Ave.
San Francisco, CA 94112 USA
ph: (415) 841-0508
ridgebackpress@mindspring.com
www.ridgebackpress.com

Publisher's Cataloging-in-Publication Data

Hillsborough, Romulus.
  Samurai sketches : from the bloody final days of the
Shogun / by Romulus Hillsborough. -- 1st ed.
  p. cm.
  Includes bibliographical references and index.
  LCCN: 00-091713
  ISBN: 0-9667401-8-1

  1. Samurai--Japan--History--Restoration, 1853-1870.
2. Japan--History--Restoration, 1853-1870.   I. Title.

DS881.3.H55 2001   952'.025
                          QBI00-742

"The sword is in the man."

A Japanese saying

A flower is cherished for its pure fragrance.
A man glories in humanity and justice.
Imprisonment brings no shame,
As long as one's heart is clearly just.

Takechi Hanpeita, July 1864
(Written on his self-portrait with brush in ink, as he languished in his jail cell)

CONTENTS

❖ LIST OF ILLUSTRATIONS ❖

(Between pages 166 and 167)

❖ ACKNOWLEDGMENTS ❖

There are many people and institutions who have contributed to the realization of this book. These include writers, historians and teachers, as well as museums and historical societies in Japan. The author is particularly indebted to those following for their invaluable inspiration, ideas, and support, without which this book would not have been possible. Names are listed alphabetically.

John Bonow, George L. Cohen, Minako Cohen, Suiken Fukunaga, Michio Hirao, Mitake Katsube, Mamoru Matsuoka, Saichiro Miyaji, Tae Moriyama, Mariko Nozaki, Tsutomu Ohshima, Kiyoharu Omino, Kan Shimosawa, David Stern, Tokyo Ryoma-kai, Hiromi Yoshikawa

❖ Note on Japanese Pronunciation ❖

The pronunciation of vowels and diphthongs are approximated as follows:

a	as in	"car"
e	as in	"pen"
i	as in	"police"
o	as in	"low"
u	as in	"sue"
ai	as in	"sky"
ei	as in	"bay"
au	as in	"now"

ii   There is no English approximation of this sound. There is a slight pause between the first "i" and the second "i".

Note that an "e" following a consonant is not a hard sound, but rather a soft one. For example, *sake* is pronounced "sa-kay," and Kobe "ko-bay."

There are no English approximations for the following sounds. They consist of only one syllable.

ryo
myo
hyo
kyo
ryu
kyu
tsu

AUTHOR'S NOTE ❖

Each individual sketch herein is a separate story in and of itself. In telling them collectively, however, it has been my wider objective to coherently, though briefly, recount the great epic which was the dawn of modern Japan. Accordingly, the reader will find that the circumstances, both historical and situational, laid out in previous sketches do much to elucidate those of subsequent ones. It is therefore recommended that the sketches be read in the sequence they appear. To provide a clearer understanding of the overall tapestry of these complicated times, I have included *A Brief Historical Background of the Meiji Restoration*. It is a summary of the historical, political, and social mind-set wherein these samurai lived and died.* Kiyoharu Omino, a distinguished Japanese historian and sword specialist, has been generous enough to write the *Introduction: On the Samurai*, which I have translated. It is a terse, insightful exposition on Japan's two-sworded class, written with the Western reader in mind and providing important information not otherwise available in the English language.

Writers of history of a distant period must depend almost entirely on recorded information, augmented perhaps by oral tradition, and aided, hopefully, by a vivid imagination. Accordingly, I hereby qualify every historical "fact" written herein with the statements "it has been written that" or "it is generally assumed that," which, for obvious reasons, I have omitted in the text.

As in my previous book, for the sake of authenticity I have placed Japanese family names before given names, and used the Chinese calendar rather than the Gregorian one to preserve the

---

*For a more detailed account of these times, the nearly fifteen years from the coming of Perry to the abdication of the last Shogun, see *RYOMA — Life of a Renaissance Samurai*, by Romulus Hillsborough.

AUTHOR'S NOTE

flavor of the mid-nineteenth century. I have romanized Japanese terms when I felt that translation would be syntactically awkward or semantically incorrect. Romanized terms other than proper nouns are italicized, except for those words, such as "samurai" and "kimono," which are included in the lexicon of modern American English. I have translated proper nouns which lend themselves favorably to an English rendering. I have not necessarily adhered to standard translations of terms which have been handed down by past writers of things Japanese. Japanese terms have not been pluralized, because their anglicization, I feel, would appall the japanized ear.

In anticipation of a common question by readers of my previous book, I have not included a bibliography because most of my references have been Japanese works. Their titles would therefore be meaningless to a readership unfamiliar with the Japanese language. Works in the English language which I have referred to include *A Diplomat in Japan* (Sir Ernest Satow), *Bushido* (Inazo Nitobe), *Samurai and Silk* (Haru Matsukata Reischauer) and *The Samurai Sword* (John Yumoto).

Unlike the first sixteen sketches, the last two sections preceding the *Historical Background* are collections of anecdotes and shorter vignettes, as their titles indicate. I have included them because I believe they warrant an English rendering, in that the spiritual design inherent in each adds to the overall tableau of the soul of the samurai which I have hoped to capture herein.

The four poems in this book, namely those by Takechi Hanpeita, Kondo Isami and Serizawa Kamo, and the quatrain on the Japanese sword cited at the beginning of the sketch titled *Cutting Test*, are my own translations. I have also provided an English rendering of the short jingle which Sakamoto Ryoma contrived at the expense of his enemies, and which appears in the sketch titled *A Natural and Overwhelming Desire*.

AUTHOR'S NOTE

For the benefit of readers who have trouble keeping track of Japanese names, I have included a brief list of main players (in order of appearance) at the beginning of each sketch, and a more detailed *Dramatis Personae* before the first sketch. To remind readers which side of the revolution these samurai represented, following their names are the letters (*L*) [(short for Loyalist) for anti-Shogunate Imperial Loyalist], (*S*) [for supporter of the Shogunate] or (*U*) [for supporter of a union between the Imperial Court and the Shogunate]. If a character's political stance is not indicated, it does not apply to these pages. The *Glossary* located before the *Index* will further help readers to recall the meanings of Japanese terms.

❖ PREFACE ❖

"The soul of the samurai lies in his sword," and to this axiom may been added, the soul of old Japan lies in the unwritten code of the samurai. "The Way of the Warrior is found in dying," states an ancient precept of samurai mores, suggesting that a noble death was the pinnacle of a samurai's life. Herein are brief sketches of samurai who preferred "to die a thousand deaths than live a life of infamy as a coward," but who believed that "to die without accomplishing one's objective was to die like a dog."

The samurai comprised the ruling class of feudal Japan, where a person's caste was determined by birthright. Below the warrior class were the peasants, the artisans and the merchants, in this order of social hierarchy. The samurai was the only member of society allowed to bear arms, and indeed it was his duty to be armed at all times. He wore two swords at his left hip, one long and one short. It is no coincidence that most, if not all, of the creators of modern Japan were adept swordsmen, nor is there any ring of irony to the fact that these men who rid their nation of its feudal shackles strictly adhered to feudalism's ethical code of honor.

All but one of the sketches herein are of actual events and people of mid-nineteenth-century Japan, during the bloody death throes of the Tokugawa Shogunate at the eve of the Meiji Restoration.* This was an age of chaos and turmoil, inner-fighting among samurai, foreign intervention, assassination and political intrigue, when the days of old Japan were coming to an end, and the dawn of a new age was upon the nation. Some of these men are great historical figures, counted among modern Japan's founding fathers. Others, though less celebrated in the

---

*The sketch titled *An Evil Woman* takes place during the decade after the fall of the Shogunate.

PREFACE

annals of Japan, are every bit as noteworthy for their unyielding devotion to their unwritten code. All are remarkable for the manner in which they lived during an age of cultural, social and political revolution. I have done my best to portray these samurai in their proper light, both for the good and the bad, as years of research indicate. Some of these sketches are concerned more with a certain tradition or mind-set among the samurai classes, than with pure history. In such instances I have taken poetic license with circumstances in order to bring each story to life, much in the spirit of the bards and poets of past ages.

My intention in writing this book has, from its very conception, been to accurately present the heart and soul of the samurai, the social and political systems of whom have, like the Japanese sword, become relics of a distant age, but the likes of whose nobility shall never again be seen in this world. In so doing, I have taken great pains not to sacrifice historical or cultural authenticity. Some readers might question the propriety of the extreme explicitness in which certain scenes of bloodshed are portrayed. Omitting these very gory descriptions would have been to overlook an aspect of these truly violent times which a realistic rendering must not ignore.

In closing, I quote Thomas Carlyle's essay *On History*.* "Under a limited, and the only practicable shape, History proper, that part of History which treats of remarkable action, has, in all modern as well as ancient times, ranked among the highest arts, and perhaps never stood higher than in these times of ours. For whereas, of old, the charm of History lay chiefly in gratifying our common appetite for the wonderful, for the unknown; and her office was but as that of a Minstrel and Story-teller, she has now farther become a Schoolmistress, and professes to

___
*This essay was published in 1830.

XV

PREFACE

instruct in gratifying." In presenting these sketches I have ventured to both instruct and gratify. I would instruct in the sense that, to the best of my knowledge, only those incidents involving foreigners* have ever before been scrutinized in English prose, and never from the unbiased perspective of the samurai involved.** If I can gratify the reader to an even partial extent of the sheer pleasure that was mine in their initial hearing, my labor in writing down these sketches will not have been lost.

Romulus Hillsborough
San Francisco
July 2000

---

*Namely, the murder of the Englishman Charles Lenox Richardson, the coincidental attack on three other Britons, and the resulting bombardment of a Japanese fiefdom by British warships.

**The murder of Richardson, portrayed in *To Cut a Foreigner*, is known in English as the Richardson Affair, while Japanese historians refer to it as the Namamugi Incident.

❖ INTRODUCTION ❖

On the Samurai

Until the Meiji Restoration in 1867, Japan was divided into some 260* feudal domains. These domains were under the military dictatorship of the central government in Edo (present-day Tokyo). The central government, known as the Bakufu, was ruled by fifteen consecutive generations of the House of Tokugawa, a samurai family. The Head of the House of Tokugawa held the title of Shogun. He was the supreme ruler of Japan.

Each domain was ruled by a feudal lord. The local affairs of the individual domains were administered by their own samurai, and each had their own governments and laws. All governmental functions were performed by the men of the warrior class, who in turn received annual stipends from their respective governments. These stipends were calculated in bushels of rice, which was produced by the peasants.

Each samurai belonged to either a feudal domain or the Bakufu. Those of the two-sworded class who belonged to neither were *ronin*, or lordless samurai.

In ancient times the Emperor ruled Japan. His power was usurped by the warrior class in the late twelfth century. From this time the samurai ruled Japan without opposition until the latter part of the nineteenth century, when a school of thought known as *Imperial Reverence* came to the fore. Proponents of *Imperial Reverence* believed that the Emperor, who resided in Kyoto, was the true and rightful ruler of Japan, and that he must be restored to his ancient seat of power.

The Tokugawa established the Bakufu in Edo in 1603.

---

*This number fluctuated between 260 and 270.

INTRODUCTION

Previously, Japan had been ruled by the Ashikaga family of samurai, and the great warlords Oda Nobunaga and Toyotomi Hideyoshi. The tumultuous era of these warlords is known as the Age of Civil Wars. In 1600, the decisive and bloody Battle of Sekigahara was waged between the two greatest powers in Japan. Some 140,000 Eastern Forces defeated 85,000 Western Forces in just one day of fighting. The commander of the Eastern Forces was the warlord Tokugawa Ieyasu. After Sekigahara, Tokugawa and his descendants ruled the Japanese nation until 1867.

During the long Age of Civil Wars, samurai who excelled in the martial arts performed brilliantly on the field of battle. Their martial achievements opened the way for their future successes. Small groups of men formed around them. These small groups gradually grew into large groups, which took over small domains.

There is an old Japanese term, "inferiors overcoming superiors," and indeed this was an age in which subordinates gained control of the domains of their leaders, and vassals overthrew their liege lords. It was also an age when a man was free to change his position in society. Anything and everything was obtainable through military force and economic power.

In 1543 a Portuguese ship* landed on the island of Tanegashima, south of Kyushu. This event foreshadowed great changes in the tides of war which had embroiled the nation, for it was then that the matchlock gun was introduced to Japan. Two of the men aboard the Portuguese ship carried harquebuses. When the feudal lord of Tanegashima witnessed one of them

---

*According to some records this was a Chinese cargo ship with Portuguese on board.

shooting game, he purchased their guns at an exorbitant price. The Japanese have a genius for reproduction, and soon matchlock guns, which were easily reproduced by Japanese swordsmiths turned gunsmiths, had spread throughout Japan.

In the mid-sixteenth century, Oda Nobunaga produced three thousand matchlock guns, forming the most powerful army in Japan. Under Nobunaga the Age of Civil Wars came to an end and Japan was unified for the first time. Nobunaga's rule, however, did not last long. He was deceived by a follower, and killed at Honnoji temple in Kyoto. Nobunaga was succeeded by Toyotomi Hideyoshi, whose reign was also short-lived. The Tokugawa, who followed Hideyoshi, ruled Japan for the next 264 years.

At the beginning of Tokugawa rule the social system of feudal Japan took shape, along with the strictly defined social hierarchy which bound people throughout life to the caste of their birth.

The samurai made up the highest rung of feudal society. Generally, they were more educated than people of the three other classes: peasant, artisan and merchant. Since the Japanese economy was based on agriculture, the peasants accounted for the greater portion of the population, while less than ten percent belonged to the samurai class. Under Tokugawa rule, certain samurai began borrowing money from wealthy merchants. As the years passed these indebted gentlemen increased in number, while certain wealthy merchants purchased the rank of samurai.

The two and a half centuries of Tokugawa rule was, with the exception of the Shimabara Rebellion in 1637,* one of relative

*The Shimabara Rebellion was an uprising of Japanese Roman Catholics. Its failure ended the Christian movement in 17th-century Japan, and bolstered the Bakufu's determination to isolate the nation from the rest of the world.

INTRODUCTION

peace. Although the samurai were a class of warriors whose original function had been to wage war, they were now required to serve in the capacity of government administrators. This was an age when brains were more valued than the sword. Accomplished swordsmen whose skills had been in high demand during the Age of Civil Wars had difficulty finding a station in life. Meanwhile, those members of the warrior class who were endowed with political acumen received the higher ranking positions.

During this peaceful era, all aspects of samurai life were governed by strict rules. Laws were proclaimed which prohibited samurai from carrying a sword with a blade over 32.76 inches long, and which required them to wear two swords — one long, one short — at all times. Throughout the lawless Age of Civil Wars, it had not been uncommon for a samurai to carry three swords.

The peaceful reign of the Tokugawa lasted for over two and a half centuries. Peace, however, had its cost, for during these halcyon days the character of the samurai gradually degenerated. A samurai from the Owari domain by the name of Asahi Bunzaemon kept a diary of samurai life for over twenty-six years. This diary contains droll accounts of members of the warrior class who had forgotten how to fight. There were instances of forgetful samurai who, having left their swords at the theater or a tea house, only realized their blunder after they had returned home. There is even the pathetic account of a samurai whose short sword was stolen right out of its sheath as he watched a popular dance performance in town.

Society was significantly influenced by the samurai's loss of their ability to fight. In times of war, swords would break and new swords would have to be made. In peaceful times, however, men did not need new swords. Many swordsmiths went out of business. Samurai no longer purchased new suits of armor, and those which they had inherited as family heirlooms they either pawned or stored away.

Having forgotten the arts of war, many samurai were repelled by the idea of using their swords on others. Execution in Japan during this time was by beheading. Since the official beheaders of the Bakufu were now reluctant to perform their grim duties, beheadings were frequently carried out vicariously by men who were inclined to do so. Eight successive generations of men by the name of Yamada Asaemon inherited the job. The Yamada family were *ronin*. They did not receive an annual stipend from a *daimyo* or the Shogun, but rather earned their livelihood by cutting off the heads of criminals. During this era of peace, men paid large sums of money to Yamada to perform tests to assess the cutting capacity of their swords. These cutting tests were conducted on the corpses of executed criminals, and, upon occasion, on live prisoners.

Indeed the Japanese sword is very sharp. It can easily sever the head from a human body, and cut through bone. During the Age of Civil Wars Japanese swords were used to penetrate the heavy iron plating of helmets, and split open the skulls beneath.

Generally, the Japanese sword will not break in battle. It is a product of over one thousand years of craftsmanship, a lethal weapon and a work of art. The beautiful curvature and wavelike tempered line of its blade was a soothing balm that calmed the heart of the samurai.

The Tokugawa banned many things, including overseas travel, Christianity and the building of large ships. As a result, with the exception of strictly regulated foreign trade in the port city of Nagasaki, Japan was virtually isolated from the rest of the world. The Nagasaki trade was limited to the Dutch and, to a lesser extent, the Chinese and Koreans.

Meanwhile, technological and economic advances in other parts of the world brought about a flourishing sea trade. Foreign whaling ships began to appear off the Japanese coast, and there were calls from various quarters for Japan to open its doors.

In 1778, a Russian ship appeared off the northern territory of Ezo (present-day Hokkaido). The Russians requested trade with Japan, but were refused. The Russians again came to Ezo in 1797. An American ship which arrived at Nagasaki in 1803 was similarly refused a request for commercial relations. In 1804, the Russian envoy N.P. Rezanov requested trade with Japan in Nagasaki, but this appeal was also rejected. In 1807, the Russians invaded an island in northern Japan, at which time they burned a Tokugawa ship. With Russia and the United States pressuring Japan to open its doors to foreign trade, the samurai finally turned their attention to foreign affairs. The Bakufu eventually yielded to outside demands in 1854, signing a treaty with the United States and ending over two and a half centuries of isolation.

Around this time two major political movements became prominent among the samurai. These were the movements of *Imperial Reverence* and *Expelling the Barbarians*. In the latter half of the 1850s, they would combine as *Imperial Reverence and Expelling the Barbarians*, the most influential movement during the final years of the Shogun's rule. Meanwhile, open-minded samurai who realized the great worth of Western science and culture espoused a policy of *Opening the Country*, which was the official policy of the Bakufu. Many of the advocates of *Opening the Country* supported Tokugawa rule, while the men backing *Imperial Reverence and Expelling the Barbarians* bitterly opposed them. Japanese society was now divided into two groups: that which supported the Tokugawa

Shogun, and that which would overthrow him.

Imperial Reverence and Expelling the Barbarians naturally developed into the *Toppling the Bakufu* movement. Opposing the enemies of the Tokugawa was a neutral group who advocated the formation of a government by the Shogunate and the Imperial Court. Theirs was known as the *Union of Court and Camp* movement.

Inner-fighting and assassination among samurai became commonplace under this extremely complicated state of affairs, the era of which is known as the *Final Years of the Bakufu*. The leading roles in the tumultuous drama of this era were played by samurai, while the people of the other three social classes looked on, so to speak, from the gallery.

As social systems weakened, so did the rule of law which had bolstered them. Lawlessness became rampant, and the state of things in Japan was reminiscent of the Age of Civil Wars. The samurai regained their long-lost belief in the power of the sword. The martial arts underwent a renaissance, fencing academies increased in number, sword production flourished, and the samurai started to carry longer swords.

This was an age when peasants who aspired to become samurai could carry two swords at their side, dress themselves appropriately, and actually join the ranks of the warrior class. Traditionally the samurai had focused their scholastic pursuits on the Chinese classics. Now men of the lower echelons of the samurai class could improve their lot in life by pursuing foreign studies.

Even as Western scholarship gained in importance, there were very few samurai who took an interest in Christianity. Rather, most men of the sword were attracted to Buddhist doctrine and Shintoism, the indigenous "Way of the Gods." And while samurai had indeed divided into contrasting ideological groups, most shared the cherished slogan "loyalty and patriotism." These men were constantly prepared to sacrifice their lives in loyal service to their liege lord and patriotic deeds for their country. A samurai's "liege lord" was his *daimyo*, his "country" his native domain.

The notion of one Japanese nation did not yet exist in the minds of these samurai. But eventually a new type of man of the warrior class emerged. Perhaps the most celebrated among them is Sakamoto Ryoma, for whom Romulus Hillsborough has coined the term "renaissance samurai."

Ryoma was a lower ranking samurai of the Tosa domain. He committed the serious crime of leaving Tosa without permission. He subsequently gained knowledge of the West under the tutelage of an elite Bakufu official. Ryoma put this knowledge to brilliant use in the pivotal role he played in the history of Japan. He was assassinated in Kyoto in 1867.

The 264-year span of Japanese history from 1603, which marked the rise to power of the first Tokugawa Shogun, to 1867, the year of the collapse of the Bakufu and the formation of the new Imperial government, is called the Edo Period. A remarkable aspect of the Edo Period was the spread of education. Private elementary schools, or "temple schools" as they were called, became popular throughout Japan. At these schools children studied reading, calligraphy and literature from age six. Most temple schools were coeducational, and some accepted only girls, in a staunchly male-oriented society. While some temple schools were limited to the offspring of the samurai, there were others which included the children of merchants, artisans and peasants. Upon completion of the elementary curriculum, which lasted about four or five years, samurai children continued on to schools of higher education, which were run by their individual feudal domains.

The spread of education served as a foundation for the great epic which was the *Final Years of the Bakufu.* The literacy rate in Japan was high, and popular reading included the Japanese translations of certain foreign books. During this age of social and political transformation younger members of the samurai class aspired to success through new ideas and knowledge. Foreign language schools were established which attracted students from throughout Japan. While many of these students were samurai, their ranks also included people from the other three classes. Meanwhile, many samurai who lacked the capacity for scholarship sought to distinguish themselves through the martial arts. Among them were the notorious assassins and terrorists of the *Final Years of the Bakufu.*

Just as Japanese society changed through the ages, the samurai differed from one historical period to the next. There is a tremendous amount of information about the samurai which could fill many volumes. I hope that this essay has helped the reader to realize that the term "samurai" connotes a social class which consisted of distinctly individual people who lived in vastly different historical periods. Romulus Hillsborough's *Samurai Sketches* takes place during the chaotic period which marked the end of the long history of the samurai. So that the reader may fully enjoy these historical sketches, I suggest they be read with an understanding of the unique circumstances in which they are set. Were the samurai who are portrayed men of the Bakufu, or did they hail from one of the 260 feudal domains? Did they support the rule of the Shogun, or were they Imperial Loyalists fighting to overthrow him? Were they from the higher echelons of samurai society, or were they of the lower ranks? How educated were they? Did these samurai rely on

INTRODUCTION

knowledge to achieve their goals, or did they resort to violence and military force?

While these sketches are indeed authentic accounts of historical figures and events, Hillsborough has written them in a literary style similar to the short story. Accordingly, the reader's perception of them will greatly depend on his or her imagination, and each reader will certainly perceive these sketches differently, depending on the subtle intricacies of his or her mind's eye. Similarly, just as the world created by Akira Kurosawa belongs distinctly to that famous director of samurai films, the world depicted by the author of *Samurai Sketches* is uniquely his own.

Kiyoharu Omino
Japanese Historian
Tokyo, Japan
July 2000

MAP OF JAPAN

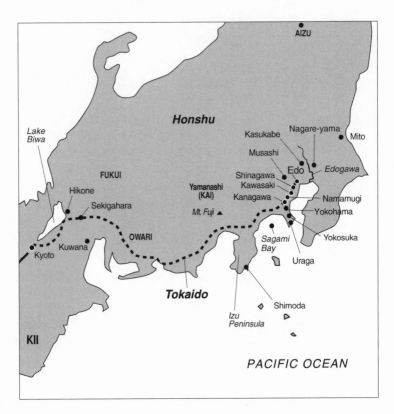

MAP OF WESTERN JAPAN

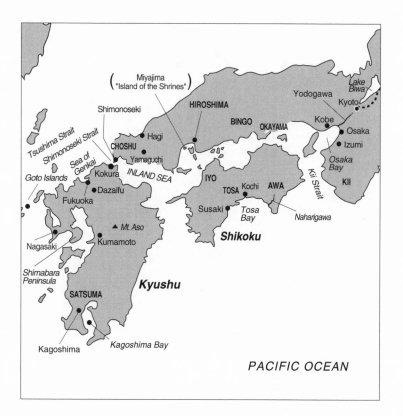

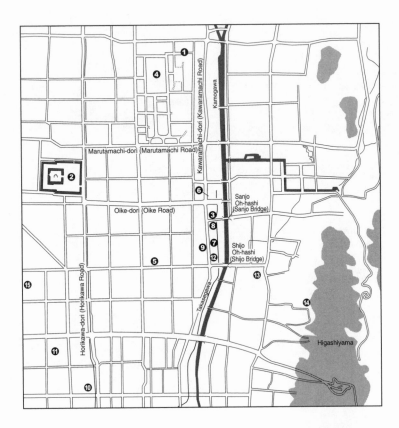

1 Site of assassination of Anenokoji Kintomo
2 Nijo Castle
3 Ikedaya
4 Imperial Palace
5 Satsuma estate
6 Choshu estate
7 Tosa estate
8 Vinegar Store

9 The Ohmiya (Sakamoto Ryoma's hideout above warehouse, and scene of his assassination)
10 Shinsengumi headquarters at temple
11 Shimabara
12 Kawaramachi
13 Gion
14 Sakamoto Ryoma's grave
15 Mibu

❖ DRAMATIS PERSONAE ❖

Akamatsu Kosaburo (*S*): A celebrated military scientist suspected by Satsuma men of spying for the Shogunate. Assassinated in Kyoto in 1867.

Anenokoji Kintomo (*L*): A leader of radicals at the Imperial Court, who was mysteriously assassinated in Kyoto in 1863.

Arima Tota (*L*): A Satsuma samurai, and vice-chief of staff of the Imperial Army who arrested Kondo Isami in 1868.

Chiba Sanako: Daughter of a celebrated sword master in Edo, who exchanged wedding vows with Sakamoto Ryoma.

Hijikata Toshizo (*S*): An expert swordsman, and vice-commander of the Shinsengumi (a shogunal police corps).

Hirai Shujiro (*L*): A Tosa samurai, and one of three lieutenants of Takechi Zuizan who was forced to commit *seppuku* in Kochi in 1863.

Hiroi Iwanosuke: A Tosa samurai who spent many years to avenge his father's murder.

Hirose Kenta (*L*): A Tosa samurai, and one of three lieutenants of Takechi Zuizan who was forced to commit *seppuku* in Kochi in 1863.

Honma Seiichiro (*L*): A *ronin* from the province of Echigo, who was assassinated by Loyalists in 1862.

Ii Naosuke (Lord Ii) (*S*): Powerful Lord of Hikone. Dictatorial Bakufu regent who authorized commercial treaties without Imperial sanction. Assassinated in Edo in 1860.

Katsu Kaishu (*S*): A faithful retainer of the Shogun. Captain of the first Japanese-manned ship to sail across the Pacific. Farsighted commissioner of the Shogun's navy who espoused international trade to save Japan from foreign subjugation. Mentor to revolutionaries who would overthrow the Shogunate.

DRAMATIS PERSONAE

Kondo Isami (aka Okubo Yamato) (*S*): An expert swordsman, and commander of the Shinsengumi (a shogunal police corps).

Masaki Tetsuma (*L*): A Tosa samurai, and one of three lieutenants of Takechi Zuizan who was forced to commit *seppuku* in Kochi in 1863.

Miura Kyutaro (*S*): A samurai and elite official of Kii, which was one of the elite Three Tokugawa Branch Houses. Suspected of masterminding assassination of Sakamoto Ryoma.

Mutsu Yonosuke (*L*): Sakamoto Ryoma's right-hand man. Leader of the "Executive Committee" to avenge Ryoma's murder.

Nakamura Hanjiro (aka "The Butcher") (*L*): A devoted follower of Saigo Kichinosuke. Notorious Satsuma swordsman who assassinated suspected shogunal spy in Kyoto in 1867.

Nakai Shogoro (*L*): A follower of Sakamoto Ryoma, and expert swordsman. Member of the "Executive Committee" to avenge Ryoma's murder.

Narahara Kizaemon (*L*): A faithful vassal of the Lord of Satsuma. Initiated attack on British subjects at Namamugi in 1862.

Okada Izo (*L*): A Tosa samurai, and notorious assassin in Kyoto under Takechi Zuizan.

Otome: An older sister of Sakamoto Ryoma.

O-ume: Mistress of Serizawa Kamo.

Saigo Kichinosuke (aka "Saigo the Great") (*L*): A Satsuma samurai, magnanimous revolutionary leader, and commander-in-chief of forces of new Imperial government.

Sakamoto Ryoma (aka Saitani Umetaro) (*L*): A Tosa samurai who fled his native domain to take part in the revolution. A devoted follower of Katsu Kaishu. Devised the plan for the Shogun's bloodless restoration of power to the Emperor. Assassinated in Kyoto in 1867.

Sawamura Sonojo (*L*): A Tosa samurai, and follower of Sakamoto Ryoma. Member of the "Executive Committee" to avenge Ryoma's murder.

Serizawa Kamo (*S*): A Mito samurai, expert swordsman, and unruly commander of the Shinsengumi (a shogunal police corps).

Shimazu Hisamitsu (Lord Hisamitsu) (*U*): Father of the nominal Satsuma *daimyo* and *de facto* lord of that clan. The most powerful man in Satsuma, which was the second largest feudal domain in Japan.

Takahashi Oden (aka "Evil Woman"): An attractive young murderess brought to the scaffold in Tokyo in 1879.

Takasugi Shinsaku (*L*): A radical leader of Choshu, who shouted blasphemy at the Shogun in Kyoto in 1863.

Takechi Zuizan (aka Takechi Hanpeita; Master Zuizan) (*L*): A Tosa samurai, master swordsman, charismatic revolutionary leader of Tosa Loyalists, and mastermind of assassinations.

Takeda Kanryusai (*S*): A squad leader of the Shinsengumi (a shogunal police corps), who was suspected of spying for Satsuma.

Tanaka Shimbe (*L*): A Satsuma samurai, and notorious assassin in Kyoto accused of Anenokoji murder.

Tanahashi Saburo (aka Matsube): Murderer of Hiroi Iwanosuke's father.

Tauchi Tomo (*S*): A rank-and-file member of the Shinsengumi (a shogunal police corps).

DRAMATIS PERSONAE

Tokugawa Iemochi (*U*): Child-Lord of Kii, who became the fourteenth Shogun.

Tokugawa Yoshinobu (Lord Yoshinobu) (*S*): A son of the Lord of Mito. The fifteenth and last Shogun, who abdicated and restored the Emperor to power in 1867.

Yamada Asaemon VII (aka "The Beheader"): The Shogunate's unofficial executioner, and the Shogun's designated sword-tester.

Yamada Asaemon VIII (aka Yoshifusa): Official executioner in Tokyo.

Yamanouchi Yodo (Lord Yodo) (*U*): Lord of Tosa, and one of Four Brilliant Lords of his time who was adamantly loyal to the Shogun. Crushed Tosa Loyalist Party, and ordered the deaths of many Tosa Loyalists.

Tamaki Yasuda: A friend of Sakamoto Ryoma's family, who in 1928 provided an eyewitness account of the aftermath of Ryoma's flight from Tosa.

Yoshida Toyo (*U*): Powerful regent to the Lord of Tosa, and nemesis of Takechi Zuizan. Assassinated in Kochi by Tosa Loyalists in 1862.

To Cut
a Foreigner

Settings

A highway near a small village, some thirty-four miles west of Edo, August 1862

Kagoshima Bay, off of Kagoshima Castletown, capital of the Satsuma domain, at the southern extremity of the island of Kyushu, summer 1863

Players

Shimazu Hisamitsu (*U*): Lord of Satsuma

Narahara Kizaemon (*L*): A Satsuma samurai

To Cut a Foreigner

"All of us were anxious to cut a foreigner. Suddenly there was a noise from behind, and I put my hand on the hilt of my sword. As I turned around I saw an Englishman on horseback holding his left side, galloping straight at me. I waited until he got close enough, then drew the blade, and in the same motion cut him about the left side of the body. A bloody piece of something fell on the grass. I suppose it was part of his entrails. I wanted to cut him again, so I chased after him. But since I was on foot, I couldn't catch up to him. I turned back and saw another foreigner galloping in my direction. I cut him about the right side with the same technique. I tell you, it was so awfully pleasant to cut them. I felt so very relieved. Fifty years have passed since then. When I think about it now, it's like a dream."

Such were the words of a retired Japanese Army major, reminiscing of his part in the brutal slaughter of an Englishman, and the wounding of two others, in August 1862. The good major had been among a retinue of Satsuma samurai escorting Shimazu Hisamitsu, lord of the Satsuma domain, from the Shogun's capital at Edo on a two-week trek to the Imperial capital at Kyoto. Lord Hisamitsu had been in Edo on a *tour de force*, accompanying two Imperial envoys who carried orders from the Imperial Court for the Shogun to report to Kyoto to discuss, among other pressing matters, "expelling the barbarians from Japan and restoring peace and order to the empire."

The Shogun was Head of the House of Tokugawa, the dynasty which had ruled Japan for two and a half centuries. For fourteen generations, the Shogun had carried the official title of Commander in Chief of the Expeditionary Forces Against the Barbarians. It had been conferred by the Emperor upon the founder of the Tokugawa dynasty, commonly known as the Tokugawa Bakufu,* at the beginning of the seventeenth century. The Shogun had borne his illustrious title well, ruling the

11

Japanese nation peacefully from his stronghold of Edo Castle, unopposed by the some 260 feudal lords throughout Japan, who, in turn, ruled peacefully over their individual domains. The halcyon days ended when, in 1858, the Tokugawa regime yielded to foreign pressure and authorized the first commercial treaties with foreign nations. A Shogun had not visited the Imperial Court in over two hundred years, until, pressed by the formidable Lord of Satsuma, the fourteenth Tokugawa Shogun yielded to the Imperial demand.

Gloating over his political victory in Edo, Lord Hisamitsu set out for the Imperial capital on the morning of August twenty-first. The Satsuma entourage projected all the pomp and pageantry warranted by a feudal lord of Hiisamitsu's rank and power. It formed a column a mile long, consisting of more than one thousand men, including seven hundred armed samurai whose xenophobic sentiments were among the strongest in Japan. With recent incidents of rude behavior by foreigners, Satsuma officials had informed the Bakufu in no uncertain terms that, if circumstances so demanded, its samurai were prepared to enforce Japanese law, "taking matters into our own hands in order to defend our honor."

The Satsuma retinue moved westward behind an advance detachment, whose purpose was to clear the way of any travelers, Japanese and foreigners alike, along the coastal Tokaido Road.** The military procession included mounted guards, riflemen, flag bearers, foot soldiers, spear bearers and halberd bearers, archers, luggage carriers, and several black lacquered palanquins borne on the shoulders of eight to a dozen men and

---

*"Bakufu" means "Shogunate." The government of the Tokugawa Shogun was referred to as the "Tokugawa Bakufu," the "Edo Bakufu," or simply the "Bakufu."

**Literally, "Eastern Sea Route," the Tokaido was the main thoroughfare between Kyoto and Edo. It stretched over 300 miles along the east coast of Honshu, the main Japanese island.

containing the persons of Lord Hisamitsu and his elite retainers. The palanquins, made of wood and split bamboo, were emblazoned in gold with the Shimazu family crest of an encircled cross. Lord Hisamitsu's palanquin, near the center of the entourage, was guarded by thirty swordsmen. At the rear of the procession, as if to flaunt his power, Hisamitsu had placed an intimidating cannon, mounted on a horse-drawn cart for all the world to see. Crowds waited silently along the roadside for a glimpse at the magnificent display. When it would finally reach their own village, the awed spectators would humbly drop to their knees, and thus remain until it had completely passed by. Such was the common respect which Japanese custom, and even law, demanded for the entourage of a *daimyo*.

Traveling on horseback from the nearby town of Kanagawa, eastward along the same strip of road, were a group of four British subjects. Silk trader William Marshall and silk inspector Woodthorpe C. Clarke, both residents of the recently established foreign settlement at Yokohama, accompanied Marshall's sister-in-law, Mrs. Margaret Borradaile of Hong Kong, and Shanghai merchant Charles Lenox Richardson. A native of London, Richardson had set up a trading business in Shanghai in 1858, perhaps because, in the words of his uncle, *"Charles was incredibly reckless and stubborn. He had to leave England because of his crazy stunts."* At age twenty-eight, Richardson had stopped at Yokohama for purposes of sightseeing, on his return to London.

It was a fine Sunday afternoon, and the four friends were on a pleasure outing to the great Taishi Temple at the nearby town of Kawasaki. On their approach to Kawasaki, they encountered a small contingent of two-sworded men, some bearing spears, others bows and arrows. Whether heedless or unaware of the grave and imminent danger ahead, the four Britons continued on their happy way. Their apparent lack of concern, if not ignorance, for their own safety seems strange in light of the fact that the Shogunate had made it a practice to inform the foreign officials at Yokohama of approaching *daimyo* entourages; and having been warned in advance of Satsuma's intolerance for impudent behavior by foreigners, the Edo government had taken special precautions to prevent any such confrontations. Whether these four Britishers had not been informed of the Satsuma schedule, or whether, as the above-cited comment of Richardson's uncle suggests, they had unwisely chosen to ignore the warning, remains a mystery. Regardless of the reason, tragedy began to unfold when the four reached the straightaway just beyond a gentle curve in the road, a short gallop to the small village of Namamugi, where the way was lined with pine trees, thirty-four miles west of Edo. At the straightaway, they saw for the first time the fast-approaching Satsuma procession, which filled the entire width of the roadway, leaving no room to pass. They also noticed the Shimazu cross, glistening gold against black, the ominous significance of which they were unaware. Startled, the four immediately slowed their pace, but did not stop and dismount, as surely they had been ordered to do. The mounted Satsuma vanguard, forming a double column, passed by without incident. Soon the entire entourage was upon them, led by a column of one hundred samurai. The foreigners, their nerves taut, finally brought their horses to a halt at the left side of the road to let the array pass by. They had positioned their horses two abreast, with Richardson and Mrs. Borradaile some ten yards beyond the two others. What happened next might be attributed to the work of an ancient Japanese god intent on cleansing the sacred land of the foreign defilement. For as the moment intensified, Mrs. Borradaile's horse lost its footing in the gutter at the side of the road. In a panicked effort to bring her horse back to the steady ground of the roadside, she accidentally got into the way of the procession, and to the grim delight of that ancient god, only twenty yards from the heavily guarded palanquin of the Lord of Satsuma. Narahara Kizaemon, a personal guard to the *daimyo* who had been walking along the rear right side of the palanquin, charged the two nearest intruders and ordered them to retreat. "Come back," Clarke called from behind. "Don't go any further," Marshall hollered. Mrs. Borradaile and Richardson tried to wheel their horses, but in their alarmed state only moved further into the procession, causing it to come to a complete halt. Taking this as a blatant insult to his lord, Narahara immediately drew his sword, slicing open the left side of Richardson's torso. A spray of blood covered Mrs. Borradaile, who, frozen in terror, screamed. Marshall and Clarke were now attacked by several other men, receiving lesser wounds to the body before galloping through the melee. Meanwhile, Richardson grabbed his bloody side with one hand, the reins with the other, and took off on a gallop. Blessed was the state of shock which had now overcome him so that he was insensible to his entrails protruding from his body, to a second blow which lacerated his rib cage as he raced through the procession, and to the bloody piece of himself that dropped on the hard-packed earth near a restaurant alongside a pine tree-lined section of the road in the small village of Namamugi. Soon Marshall caught up with Richardson, who now fell to the ground by an open-air tea booth at the side of the road, near a canal bordering a small field. But Marshall, himself badly wounded, judged that his friend's life could not be saved, and so turned back to save his own. He rejoined Clarke and Mrs. Borradaile in Kanagawa, about four miles from the scene of the slaughter, where they sought refuge at the American Consulate. Clarke had received a deep wound to his left shoulder, but, like Marshall, survived the attack. Mrs. Borradaile, though covered with Richardson's blood, was unscathed, save a portion of her long hair which had been cut off by an outraged samurai.

As the village carpenter's wife watched in horror from under the eaves of her thatched house, five Satsuma samurai approached the prostrate man, who was struggling to drag his butchered body toward the canal. "Water," he gasped, and, in a vain attempt to escape, tried to get up. But the five samurai now dragged him into the field so that he wheezed in pain, and the poor woman put her hand to her mouth for fear that they might notice her. When one of the men drew his short sword, crying "mercy of the samurai," the woman thought her heart would burst in her chest. After the man delivered the *coup de grace* to Richardson's neck, then stabbed him through the heart, the five samurai quit the scene, and the carpenter's wife rushed into her house.

Not a soul remained near the body, save Richardson's chestnut horse, which lingered nearby, covered with its rider's blood. The carpenter's wife returned momentarily, carrying several old straw mats. She looked nervously around her to make sure that the two-sworded men had not returned, then slowly walked into the field. Now she stood over the bloody corpse which lay under the shade of a tree. One side of the torso had been sliced wide open, and the chest ripped apart muscle and bone so that the lungs and stomach were visible. The intestines protruded through an opening which extended from the side of the torso to the back. The left portion of the neck had been severed from the body. A wide hole in the chest extended into the heart. The left hand had been severed at the wrist, save a thin strip of skin. As the carpenter's wife looked into the face of the foreigner, the black beard covered with gore, the mouth agape, the dead eyes filled with terror, she was simultaneously struck by feelings of pity and disgust. The face and head were unscathed, so that the strange features were apparent. She was stunned by the weird blue eyes, thick lips, heavy eyebrows protruding over the long aquiline nose, the wide forehead and the pale complexion. The body was much larger than any she had ever seen, the clothes peculiar. Over these past two or three years she had indeed seen numerous foreigners coming and going along the busy thoroughfare, but this was the first time she had ever seen one up close. She uttered a short prayer, covered the body with the mats, then hurried back to the safety of her home.

On the night of the incident, at his lodging along the way, Lord Hisamitsu summoned Narahara Kizaemon, the guard who had initiated the attack. When asked by an aide of the *daimyo* why he had drawn his sword on the unarmed foreigners, Narahara replied, "As a personal guard to the Lord of Satsuma, it is my duty to see to it that such impudence does not become a common occurrence. Had the foreigners actually harmed the procession, I would have taken responsibility by committing *seppuku*. Fortunately, however, I was able to cut one of them down before they could do any real harm." Narahara would demonstrate his readiness to die by his own sword when, three years later, he would disembowel himself at the Satsuma estate in Kyoto.

The whole affair incited outrage among the foreign community in Japan, particularly the British Legation. The British demanded that the Bakufu order Satsuma to surrender Richardson's murderers. Satsuma refused on the grounds that ancient custom and even law empowered their samurai to cut down anyone who interrupted an entourage of their *daimyo*. "If you continue to insist that we surrender even one of our brave men," they said, "you will have to arrest us one and all." In the face of Satsuma's staunch defiance, the Shogunate could do little more than warn that clan of rumors that the British were planning to send a squadron of warships to Satsuma, to settle the matter themselves. Indeed, the British government was neither to be constrained by the xenophobic sentiments of Satsuma, nor appeased by the feeble entreaty of Edo that it was unable to force Satsuma to turn over Richardson's murderers. Rather, the British demanded that indemnities be paid to the family of Richardson and to the British subjects who had been injured in the attack, and that those responsible for the crime be arrested and executed in the presence of British officers.

*　　　　　　　*　　　　　　　*

By the following summer the British had wearied of negotiations with Bakufu representatives in Edo. Near the end of June, a squadron of seven heavily armed British warships steamed into the bay at Kagoshima, the castletown and nerve center of Satsuma, to present Great Britain's final demands to that clan, and, if these demands were not accepted, to punish this second largest Japanese fiefdom. The British were met by an army of Satsuma samurai, who watched from the batteries along the coast and the lookout posts in the mountains above, and prepared to rain cannonade upon the intruders.

Before they would open fire, however, Satsuma tried to convince the principal British officers to land for negotiations in person, rather than in writing as the British had proposed. If the British would still not listen to reason, Satsuma intended to take the British officers hostage. But when the British made it clear they were not to be duped, the two samurai who had murdered Richardson, feeling the burden of responsibility for the dangerous situation at hand, devised drastic measures. *"Since we were unable to convince them to land, we came up with the daring plan to board their flagship, immediately kill all of their officers, cut down everyone else on board, and seize the ship,"* a Satsuma man would recall three decades later. After exchanging a parting cup of *sake* with their *daimyo*, ninety-eight swordsmen boarded sixteen small boats. They were dressed as peddlers who would sell watermelon and peaches to the British, and to a man had resolved to accomplish their mission or die.

"It was a bold conception, and might have been successful but for the precautions taken on our side," reported Ernest Satow, interpreter to the British minister in Japan, who witnessed the event from the deck of a British warship. *"Only two or three were permitted into the Admiral's cabin, while the marines kept a vigilant eye on the retinue who remained on the quarter deck."*

"Since we thought it would be useless to kill common sailors," the Satsuma man recalled, *"we left without accomplishing our purpose. When I look back upon it now, it seems like so much child's play."*

"Child's play" was not the British evaluation of Satsuma's actions. Five days after their arrival at Kagoshima Bay, and with the last-ditch negotiations having failed, the British seized three Satsuma steamers, and pandemonium ensued. Amidst the downpour and bluster of a powerful typhoon, Satsuma opened fire at noon with eighty-three cannon from ten batteries along the coast. The first shot hit the deck of the flagship *Euryalus*, decapitating the captain. The British retaliated by looting and burning the seized Satsuma ships, and firing upon the coastline with their superior Armstrong guns.* *"It was an awful and magnificent sight,"* wrote Satow, *"the sky all filled with a cloud of smoke lit up from below by the pointed masses of pale fire."*

The Satsuma men fought well. During the three and a half hours of battle, they had damaged most of the British ships, killed eleven of the enemy and wounded dozens more. Satsuma, however, suffered even greater losses. It was completely outgunned by the British Armstrongs, which had a firing range four times greater than the Satsuma cannon. The coastal batteries were totally destroyed, scores of samurai and townspeople killed, and a good portion of the buildings in Kagoshima Castletown burned to the ground.

The British left Kagoshima Bay the following day, satisfied they had taught Satsuma a hard lesson, as indeed they had. In fact, their defeat to the British served as a rude awakening to the warriors of Satsuma, who, with their counterparts in Choshu, would over the following four years lead the revolution to overthrow the Tokugawa Shogunate. Satsuma now realized that their

---

*Armstrongs were state-of-the-art breech-loading, rifled cannon. They shot further and more accurately, and reloaded much faster, than the muzzle-loading smooth bore guns used by Satsuma.

inferior weaponry was no match for the modern artillery and warships of the West. They would throw off their xenophobic sentiments, in name if not in spirit, and shortly after concluded a peace agreement with Great Britain. Satsuma acquiesced to pay the indemnities for the Namamugi Incident. They even went so far as to agree to punish those guilty of the murder, although they never would. Satsuma now employed British assistance to modernize their military, and from this time on, and to the dismay of Edo, became Great Britain's close ally. The British, meanwhile, had correctly assessed that the future rulers of the Japanese nation did not reside within the Shogun's stronghold at Edo, but in the remote castletowns of Satsuma and Choshu.

A Mortal
Enemy

Settings

Kochi Castletown, capital of the Tosa domain, on the southern coast of the island of Shikoku, 1855

Mountainous region in province of Kii, some forty miles south of Osaka, June 1863

Players

Hiroi Iwanosuke: A Tosa samurai intent on avenging his father's murderer

Tanahashi Saburo (aka Matsube): Murderer of Iwanosuke's father

Sakamoto Ryoma (*L*): A Tosa samurai who fled his native domain to take part in the revolution. A devoted follower of Katsu Kaishu.

Katsu Kaishu (*S*): A faithful retainer of the Shogun, farsighted commissioner of the Shogun's navy, and mentor to revolutionaries who would overthrow the Shogun's government

A Mortal Enemy

*The desire to right a wrong is universal. To the samurai, reveng-ing*a wrong done one's country,** liege lord, parent, or other-wise superior was often his sole means of realizing justice in an unjust world; and it was always his responsibility as demanded by the unwritten code which governed his very life.*

The practice of "striking down a mortal enemy" was a sanc-tioned institution in samurai society. Although there were only few instances in which official permission was granted for mur-der, it was nevertheless a basic tenet of the warrior's code that the victim of an unjustifiable crime had the right to be avenged. A crime against a liege lord was avenged by his vassals, against a father by his sons, against an elder brother by those younger. But who would avenge a crime committed against the entire Japanese nation by a decrepit and corrupt government? The self-assigned task fell to an outlaw from the Tosa clan who would overthrow the Tokugawa Bakufu.

The year was 1855, and Hiroi Iwanosuke had just been informed that his father had suddenly died. Iwanosuke's father had been a samurai in the service of the Lord of Tosa. He had been fishing in a river which ran through Kochi Castletown, the capital of the Tosa domain. He was on his way home, and had just finished paddling his boat to the riverbank. Suddenly a drunken man approached. "Bring me to the other side of the river," he demanded. When the fisherman refused, the drunken man drew his sword. A skirmish ensued. The fisherman lost his footing, fell into the river and drowned.

---

*It is noteworthy that revenge was not justified for wrongs done to oneself, including one's wife and children.

**In feudal Japan the term "country" did not connote "Japan," but, rather, was synonymous with "fiefdom" or "clan." Thus, the country of a Satsuma man was Satsuma, of a Tosa man Tosa, of a Choshu man Choshu, and so on.

Iwanosuke immediately set out to discover the circumstances of his father's death. He found out that a certain Tanahashi Saburo was to blame. He reported this to the authorities. Tanahashi was arrested. When it was determined that Tanahashi had not intentionally killed Iwanosuke's father, but was nevertheless responsible for his death, he was stripped of his samurai status and banished from Tosa. Iwanosuke was outraged that the life of his father's murderer had been spared. But when the Hiroi family line was abolished as punishment for the late patriarch's "careless behavior unbecoming of a samurai," Iwanosuke resolved to kill Tanahashi.

In the dead of winter of the following year the young samurai embarked on a journey to hunt down his irreconcilable foe. He left Tosa without permission, which, of course, was a crime. He was arrested soon after, taken back to Tosa, and confined to a village in the countryside. After three years Iwanosuke was released, and at age twenty-one, returned to the castletown. At Kochi he took up the study of *kenjutsu*. After four years of hard training, never once forgetting his ultimate objective, he was granted official permission to travel to other parts of Japan to pursue his study in the way of the sword. When Iwanosuke left Tosa in February 1863, now with an official passport in hand, he set out again to find his father's murderer.

Iwanosuke traveled across the island of Shikoku, but could find no sign of Tanahashi. He crossed the Kii Strait to the main island of Honshu, and traveled northeastward to Kyoto, but still to no avail. Eventually he ran out of money, so that by the time that he arrived at the mercantile capital of Osaka he was destitute.

Just as Iwanosuke despaired of ever finding his mortal enemy, he happened across a group of fellow Tosa samurai. These were Sakamoto Ryoma[*] and several others. They had left

---

[*]For a complete and detailed analysis of the life and times of Sakamoto Ryoma, see *RYOMA — Life of a Renaissance Samurai*.

Tosa without permission to fight in the revolution to overthrow the Bakufu. They said they had come to Osaka to make preparations for the establishment of a private naval academy under the tutelage of Katsu Kaishu. But Katsu was commissioner of the Tokugawa Navy, and Iwanosuke was confused. "I thought Katsu was a traitor who has sold out to the barbarians," he said to Ryoma. "How can you vow to overthrow the Bakufu, and at the same time work under one of its top officials?" Iwanosuke shared the sentiments of all young hotbloods from Tosa, who would overthrow the Shogun's government and expel the foreigners from Japan.

Iwanosuke had not yet realized that his own struggle to avenge his father's murder was but a scaled-down version of Ryoma's greater quest. Sakamoto Ryoma was a renowned swordsman. He had served as the head of the elite Chiba Dojo in Edo, where six years before he had been initiated in the Hokushin-Itto Style of fencing. He was the former right-hand man of Takechi Zuizan, the revered kingpin of the Tosa Loyalist Party. Ryoma was now the leader of the young rebels who served under the brilliant navy commissioner. He was also a once and future outlaw. He had fled Tosa in March of the previous year because he hated the restraints of feudalism. Throwing off these restraints, he had become a *ronin*, a lordless samurai, an outlaw. "*A samurai receiving a stipend from his lord,*" Ryoma often said, "*is like a bird being kept in a cage. If I don't feel in my heart that something is right, I get rid of it like I would an old cage.*" The old cage to Ryoma was his native Tosa. Soon after fleeing Tosa, Ryoma found himself destitute. His only possession of value was his sword. He pawned the silver pommel for some gold coins, before making his way to the dangerous streets of Kyoto. Here he visited the estate of the renegade Choshu clan, whose men sheltered him as one of their own. The Choshu men informed Ryoma that Yoshida Toyo, the powerful regent to the Lord of Tosa, had been assassinated in Kochi, and that the assassination had been masterminded by Takechi Zuizan. Yoshida had been murdered just after Ryoma had fled, and now he was wanted for a crime which he did not commit. The Choshu men convinced Ryoma to remain in the safe confines of their Kyoto estate. But soon he began to feel like he had traded his cage in Tosa for the one provided by his friends from Choshu. He told them that he had not fled Tosa just to go into hiding. He must get involved in the revolution, he said, and contribute to the overthrow of the Bakufu, which he likened to *"cleaning up Japan once and for all."* He was a lover of freedom — the freedom to act, the freedom to think, the freedom to be. These were the ideals that drove Ryoma on his dangerous quest for salvation, the salvation of Japan.

Ryoma told the Choshu men that he would travel to the Shogun's capital. "At Edo you'll be able to put your sword to some use by cutting down the traitor Katsu Kaishu," one of them had urged. Ryoma had never heard the name. But when his friends informed him that two years previously Katsu had commanded the first Japanese-manned ship to sail across the Pacific, and that he was one of Japan's leading advocates of conducting free trade with foreign nations, Ryoma determined to meet him.

Ryoma visited Katsu's home in Edo one night in October 1862. Some claim that he had intended to kill Katsu as a traitor. Others suggest that he had sought out the navy commissioner because of his own fascination with things maritime, particularly the modern warships of the West. Far from intending to kill Katsu, they argue, Ryoma was filled with admiration for this pioneer of the Japanese navy. What is certain is that the unruly outlaw was mesmerized by the elite Bakufu official. Katsu discoursed to Ryoma of the dire necessity of developing a navy and conducting free trade. He argued that Japan must continue to trade with the Western powers if it hoped to defend itself against them. Japan must import technology from Europe and the United States, he said. Katsu told Ryoma of the overwhelming naval and commercial power of Great Britain, by which that nation had brought China to its knees. "No matter how much we rant and rave about keeping the barbarians out, we just don't have the means to do so," he declared. To develop these means Katsu proposed that men throughout Japan study naval science, and acquire the maritime skills required to build a modern navy. "That includes you," Katsu told him. The navy commissioner's ideas confused the fugitive. Only the sons of elite government officials were permitted to study naval science. Even if such privileges were extended to lower ranking samurai from the remote provinces, Ryoma was an outlaw, suspected of murder and wanted for fleeing his clan. But when Katsu invited Ryoma to work with him to achieve these lofty goals, he readily accepted. The outlaw who would overthrow the Tokugawa Bakufu would first become the devoted follower of one of its leaders. Ryoma soon set about recruiting other Tosa men into Katsu's service. Those he recruited were rebels like himself, who had fled Tosa to support the cause of overthrowing the Shogunate. "Come work with me under the greatest man in Japan," he told them. "We are going to develop a navy."

Some people said Ryoma was crazy. Others called him a traitor. "A lot of people talk about *Expelling the Barbarians* these days," he told Iwanosuke, upon their chance meeting in Osaka. "But we simply don't have the means to do so. Katsu-sensei says we must open the country in order to acquire the proper military and industrial technology to defend ourselves. We need warships. We need a powerful navy. But first of all we need a naval academy to train ourselves."

"But Katsu is the..."

"I know what he is," Ryoma interrupted. "He's the greatest man in Japan. He's also the most knowledgeable man when it comes to operating a modern warship." Ryoma paused, then scowled. "Instead of criticizing people, why don't you join us?"

Iwanosuke returned the scowl with a frown, then told

Ryoma of his failed attempt to avenge his father's murder. "But I must find my mortal enemy and kill him," he said, "or die trying."

"I see," said Ryoma, also frowning. "I know exactly how you feel."

"How could you?" Iwanosuke said bitterly. "Have you ever had a mortal enemy?"

"Yes," Ryoma replied, slowly folding his arms at his chest.

Ryoma felt that the Bakufu was only concerned for its own welfare, at the expense of the rest of Japan. Although it had ruled the nation peacefully for two and a half centuries, its institutions had become old and decrepit. The times were changing. The Bakufu had started losing its ability to rule ten years ago, when Commodore Perry's flotilla of warships had first come to Japan. Xenophobic samurai throughout the archipelago, particularly those of Choshu, Satsuma and Tosa, had been up in arms since the Bakufu had yielded to the foreign demands to open the nation. The barbarians must be expelled, they demanded, and the Bakufu destroyed. The xenophobes, who now called themselves "Imperial Loyalists," claimed that the rule of the nation must be restored to the Emperor in Kyoto, the rightful ruler of Japan. Ryoma had been among the xenophobes, but recently his eyes had been opened by Katsu Kaishu. While he still shared the Loyalists' goal to overthrow the government, he now realized that the only way to expel the foreigners and save Japan from subjugation would be to develop a strong navy and conduct international trade.

"I think I know someone who can help you," Ryoma told Iwanosuke. "After you've taken care of your business, you can help us with ours."

"But who could possibly help me?" Iwanosuke asked despondently.

"The greatest man in Japan," Ryoma replied.

Presently Ryoma introduced Iwanosuke to his mentor. Katsu

admired Iwanosuke's filial loyalty. He sympathized with his plight. He also composed a short letter, addressed to local government officials throughout Japan, requesting their assistance in "helping my new recruit to avenge his father's murder." With this letter in his pocket, and disguised as a common coolie, Iwanosuke set out with renewed hopes of finding Tanahashi.

Iwanosuke eventually heard about a man called Matsube who claimed to be from Tosa. Matsube was a day laborer. When drunk he was known to boast about having killed a man. Further investigation indicated that this day laborer had been a samurai of the Tosa clan, and that his former name was Tanahashi. He was now in the province of Kii, some forty miles from Osaka, where he was engaged in the construction of shore batteries defending the coast.

Accompanied by several of Ryoma's men and armed with his short and long swords, Iwanosuke went directly to the place on the coast of Kii, where the said batteries were under construction. But his hopes of finally accomplishing his goal were soon dashed. He was informed that the man who called himself Matsube had been arrested by the Kii authorities for a certain wrongdoing. Iwanosuke was not told, however, that the arrest had been arranged by Katsu Kaishu himself, as a precautionary measure to prevent the sudden disappearance of his new recruit's enemy. When Iwanosuke subsequently found out that Tanahashi was to be officially expelled from the province of Kii, he acted accordingly.

In the late morning of June second, the man who called himself Matsube was led under armed guard to a bridge, in a mountainous region at the northwestern border of Kii. Waiting here since dawn were Iwanosuke, several other Katsu recruits, and thousands of local people who had come to watch the spectacle.

As soon as the prisoner was released by his guards, and crossed over the border into the province of Izumi, his mortal enemy was upon him. Hoping to trick Tanahashi into revealing his true identity, Iwanosuke grabbed him by the hair, screaming, "You're real name is Yoshiharu, and you were born in Tosa."

"I don't know anyone by that name," the man said.

"Then what's your real name?"

"Tanahashi Saburo."

His mortal enemy having fallen for the ploy, Iwanosuke identified himself as his father's son. "And now you will die," he screamed, thrusting a sheathed sword at Tanahashi. The startled man accepted the weapon. He drew the blade, but to no avail. The psychological advantage afforded by nine years of pent up hatred was overwhelming. Iwanosuke severed Tanahashi's right hand at the wrist. The ensuing screams of pain were drowned out by the cheering of Iwanosuke's several comrades, and the surrounding throngs. When Iwanosuke cut his enemy across the side of the head, he was overcome by a surging sense of pleasure such as he had never before known. Tanahashi staggered, and Iwanosuke immediately cut him alongside the body. Now the bloodied man collapsed, and Iwanosuke delivered the death blow to the throat.

Later that day Iwanosuke surrendered himself to the chief magistrate. Routine inspection, not to mention the good offices of the influential navy commissioner, confirmed that Iwanosuke had acted within his rights, and that justice had been served. Iwanosuke now returned to Tosa to report that he had killed his father's enemy. "I have wasted the first half of my life with a burning desire for revenge," he told the authorities. "I now intend to make a new start, and be of use to the nation under the guidance of Katsu Kaishu." But Iwanosuke's health had badly deteriorated over the long years of hardship he had endured to accomplish his revenge. He died of illness just two years later at age twenty-seven.

Courage

Setting
A crowded barroom in San Francisco's notorious Barbary Coast, March 1860

Player
Katsu Kaishu (*S*): A retainer of the Shogun, and captain of the first Japanese-manned ship to sail across the Pacific Ocean

Courage

To the samurai, degree of courage was not measured by one's readiness to draw one's sword, nor were fearlessness nor blind bravery qualities of a truly courageous man. Courage, rather, was a quality inseparable from strength of mind and fortitude of spirit. "I keep the hilt of my sword so tightly fastened to the scabbard that I'd have trouble just drawing the blade," bantered a champion of the philosophy that a truly courageous man might let himself be cut before cutting someone else. The banterer was Katsu Kaishu, loyal retainer of the Tokugawa Shogun, founder of the Japanese Navy, adept swordsman, mentor of revolutionaries, and the man whose farsighted courage saved the Japanese capital from the flames of civil war.

The large beveled glass mirror behind the dark wooden bar reflected the dim gaslight in the barroom, frequented by sailors from five continents, jaded miners from the Nevada silver fields, harlots, gun-toting hoodlums and other assorted riffraff, and, upon occasion, gentlemen from various walks of life.

The mild-mannered, Oriental gentleman who sat alone drinking a glass of beer at a table at the back of the crowded barroom on this particular evening in March 1860 struck the woman as unlike anyone she had ever seen. The woman was a harlot who worked the bars which lined back streets with names like "Murder Point," "China," "Moketown" and "Dead Man's Alley." Owing to the demands of her profession, she was perhaps younger than her appearance suggested, and substantially more perceptive of her surroundings. She had coarse features — a wide, slightly jutting forehead, heavy brows, watery blue eyes, long yellow hair braided into a ponytail, and fleshy red lips. She was dressed as her profession required — a tight-fitting red dress embroidered with black lace, and cut low around her broad shoulders and large, protruding breasts. As a matter of course she always carried a derringer, small enough to tuck neatly and out of sight inside her dress. As her occupation brought her into intimate contact with a wide variety of men, she had, of necessity, developed an uncanny ability to readily assess the character of those she encountered.

Not so, however, for this particular Oriental gentleman. He was neatly dressed in a light blue kimono, pleated gray trousers and a black silk jacket adorned here and there with white images of a four-petaled flower in a circle. Thrust through his silken sash at his left hip were two swords, one much longer than the other. The swords were set in black lacquered sheaths, and their ivory sharkskin hilts were bound tightly with dark blue silk cord. Just under five feet tall, and of a slight, wiry physique, the exotic gentleman was, with the exception of a Chinese sailor the harlot had once entertained, the smallest man she had ever seen. Although she could not know his exact age, she aptly estimated that he was around thirty-seven. The lady found the Oriental gentleman attractive — his light complexion, slightly aquiline nose, thin lips and small jaw produced an aristocratic air, and his full head of black hair was oiled and tied neatly in a topknot. But more than his exterior features, it was the uncanny inner strength radiating from the Oriental gentleman's dark eyes which impressed her.

The Oriental gentleman was a samurai who hailed from the Japanese capital of Edo. He was a direct retainer of the House of Tokugawa, the dynasty which had ruled Japan for some two and a half centuries, and whose head bore the title of Shogun. The samurai had recently sailed from Yokohama to San Francisco as captain of the *Kanrin Maru*. The thirty-seven-day journey across the Pacific was a feat as daunting as it was challenging. The *Kanrin Maru* was a tiny Dutch-built triple-masted wooden schooner, originally named the *Japan*, which had been designed to sail only in coastal waters. By Western standards, the all-Japanese crew were novices in the art of navigation, and theirs was the first Japanese expedition to the Western world. Perhaps equally deterring of a transpacific journey for the

diminutive sea captain, who two years hence would be appointed to the powerful post of commissioner of the Tokugawa Navy,
was his propensity for seasickness. So fragile was his physical
constitution that when his tiny vessel nearly capsized in stormy
seas, he became too ill to leave his cabin.

The *Kanrin Maru* was the escort ship to the first Japanese
delegation to the United States. The delegation had been dispatched by the Shogunate to ratify a commercial treaty between
the two countries. The *Kanrin Maru* had left Japan three days
before the delegation, which sailed to Washington D.C. aboard
the very seaworthy *U.S.S. Powhatan*, commanded by a U.S.
Navy captain and his very competent crew.

Protocol, and indeed common sense, demanded that the captain of the escort ship to the Japanese delegation remain out of
harm's way with the rest of his countrymen at the hotel on
Montgomery Street at the city's center to await the arrival of the
U.S.S. Powhatan. But this particular samurai was a maverick
within his government and a misfit within the rigid social structure of feudal Japan. He despised the outdated social structure
whereby one's lot in life was predetermined by birthright, and
whereby men of ability were not allowed to participate in government if their fathers were among the lower castes.

As Katsu Kaishu had been born into the impoverished
household of a low-ranking samurai, he seemed destined to
spend his entire life working as a petty official. But with the
coming of Commodore Perry in 1853, and the subsequent
demands made by the foreigners that Japan be opened to the
rest of the world, this farsighted samurai composed a brilliant
letter of advice to the Bakufu. The letter proposed that the
Bakufu break an age-old tradition, and go beyond social class
to recruit men of ability for these very pressing times. It also
advised that Japan begin international trade, using the profits
thereby to build a modern navy in order to defend itself against
subjugation by the Western powers. Although the ranks of the
Shogun's government were filled with men of mediocre ability

who had attained their posts due to nothing more than birthright, such was not the case for the entire Edo elite. And fortunately for Katsu — and indeed the future of Japan — his talents caught the attention of the most progressive officials in these very troubled times. Katsu was subsequently sent to study under Dutch naval experts in the port city of Nagasaki. It was here that he obtained the knowledge and skills that enabled him to stand at the helm of the *Kanrin Maru.*

Katsu snickered at the petty disdain which his comrades displayed one evening when he left the safe confines of their hotel for the unpredictable streets of San Francisco. "Don't those idiots want to see how Americans live?" he thought, as he bowed slightly to the bellman, and a chilly ocean breeze pierced his fine silk kimono. "Unless we understand our adversaries, we can never defeat them." Over the following several years Katsu would be counted among the most powerful men in the Shogunate, but now he was curious to see how the common people lived. He had learned that in the United States the poor had the same rights as the rich, and that even a farmer or a merchant could rise to the pinnacle of power. He was fascinated by what he had recently learned about American democracy, the *Constitution of the United States*, and the *Bill of Rights*. He even harbored the preposterous idea of somehow introducing these very foreign ideas into Japan. That he jeopardized his personal safety by venturing outside unescorted and virtually unarmed, in search of the common man, did not concern this samurai, who over the next several years would survive numerous attempts on his life by radicals intent on overthrowing the government; who would recruit from among these radicals men to whom he would impart the arts of naval warfare and maritime navigation; who three years hence would risk a possible death sentence by advising the Shogun to abdicate in order to avoid a bloody civil war; and who would be one of only a few in the government to command the reverence and trust of the revolutionaries even as they pounded the last nail into the coffin of the

Tokugawa Shogunate.

From his hotel, the Oriental gentlemen headed north along Montgomery Street, because he had heard that in the northern part of the city he might most readily observe the common man. This main thoroughfare was lined with gaslights, so that he easily found his way to a street of crowded bars, dancing halls, gambling dens and other houses of ill repute. Certainly the discerning samurai in the service of the Shogun was well aware of the dangers lurking in the mean streets of San Francisco's notorious Barbary Coast, where "No decent man was in safety to walk the streets after dark."[*] Presently he entered the crowded barroom, which he was satisfied to see filled with so-called common men — common in a town where murder was a daily occurrence. Standing alone at the bar was a hulking vulgarian with a thick red beard and a gaping scar extending from his left cheekbone to the base of his jaw. He was dressed as a miner — blue denim trousers covered with filth, a red plaid shirt, a tattered broad-rimmed hat, a pistol at his right hip, an imposing bowie knife at his left, and a pair of heavy black boots. The hulking vulgarian now cast a look of disgust at the harlot, as she seated herself at the table with the Oriental gentleman. "What'cha sittin' over thar with that li'l monkey fer?" he blustered. "I otta skin 'im like a jackrabbit."

What the hulking vulgarian with the thick red beard did not realize was that the diminutive Oriental gentleman whom he had mistaken for a simian cousin understood very little English. Nor could he know that this two-sworded gentleman had been initiated in the art of *kenjutsu* at the fencing academy of Shimada Toranosuke, one of the most reputable sword masters in the Shogun's capital. During wintertime, in addition to rigorous daily practice sessions, Master Shimada imposed upon his devoted pupil a most severe form of mental training. Each night

[*]From *The Annals of San Francisco*, by Frank Soulé, John H. Gihon and James Nisbet

Katsu would go alone to a Buddhist temple, wearing only a thin cotton robe, despite the biting cold. Upon arriving at the temple, he would seat himself on the foundation stone of the sanctuary. *"At first, all alone in* the dead of night," Katsu recalled a half century later, *"in the temple precincts set in a deep dark forest, I couldn't help but feel somewhat frightened. The sound of the wind filled me with dread, so that the hair all over my body stood on end. And it seemed that one of the huge trees might come crashing down upon my head at any time."* Overcoming his fear, Katsu would meditate with eyes closed, *"to cultivate courage."* Next he would take up his wooden sword for an exhausting training session. Upon completing his first set of drills, he would resume his meditation. At the break of dawn, having repeated the process four or five times, he would return to the academy of his fencing master for the daily practice.

Master Shimada urged his pupils to practice Zen in order to learn the secrets of the art of fencing. Katsu began his Zen training at age twenty. Each morning, in the cold darkness before dawn, the pupils would assemble in the temple hall. Speaking was strictly prohibited, as were yawning, coughing, sneezing and all other forms of noise. Barefoot and clad in short cotton robes and trousers, the pupils would form perfectly straight rows, four or five abreast. They would kneel on the bare wooden floor, assuming a proper sitting posture — legs and feet tucked underneath, back straight, eyes looking ahead and slightly downward, hands resting atop the thighs. The pupils were forbidden to move from this position for a certain period of time — perhaps one hour, perhaps two, occasionally three — regardless of the pain in their cramped, burning muscles. The only sound was that of their breath flowing in and out of their bodies, until the silence was inevitably broken by a sudden and sharp crack of the Zen priest's hard wooden stave upon the shoulder of one who had momentarily lost his proper posture, emitted a sound, flinched, or in any other way violated the severe code of Zen training.

Violation of the code was not always easily detected. "*You might be thinking about money, about women, about good food or any other number of things. But if you lost your concentration, you were sure to be hit so hard that you would fall right over.*" Katsu continued his study of Zen for nearly four years. "*There was a period in my life when assassins were always giving me a hard time. But through my training I developed the courage and nerve to subdue them.*"

When subduing an assailant was impossible, Katsu would opt for a quick escape. "*In case escape was not feasible, I was always resolved to give up my life.*" In August 1866, the Shogun's forces suffered a series of humiliating defeats at the hands of the revolutionary Choshu Army. Navy Commissioner Katsu Kaishu subsequently traveled alone, dressed as a petty samurai and without a single bodyguard, to the Island of the Shrines in the domain of Hiroshima to negotiate terms of peace with the enemy. He was well aware that the Choshu men were out for nothing short of Tokugawa blood, and as a special emissary of the House of Tokugawa he might very well be assassinated. Shortly after landing on the island, Katsu was confronted by a patrol of Choshu soldiers, each armed with a rifle.

"Halt!" one of them ordered, training his rifle at Katsu. "Identify yourself."

Katsu immediately sensed that if he tried to cover up his thick Edo accent, he might very well be shot as a spy. But if he were to reveal his true identity, he might be killed anyway. "My name is Katsu," he said calmly, gesturing for the man at the front of the patrol to point his rifle downward. "Katsu Kaishu, from Edo."

"Katsu Kaishu!" the Choshu man shouted. There was not a samurai in all of Japan who did not know the name. "You mean the Katsu Kaishu?" he sneered. "Of course, we can see from your elaborate clothes, and your large escort that you are none other than the commissioner of the Tokugawa Navy."

Katsu continued speaking in the same calm voice. "If you're

going to shoot, please take careful aim and get the job done as quickly as possible. You see, it'll be shameful enough dying of a gunshot wound, when the only honorable way for a samurai to die is by the sword. But dying slowly in such a manner would be too much to bear."

Something in Katsu's demeanor, perhaps his resolve to die, must have convinced the leader of the patrol. No sooner had he finished speaking than the leader suddenly gasped, "You are Katsu-sensei!" He dropped to his knees, and to the dismay of his subordinates, bowed his head to the ground.

"Another beer, please," the samurai now said to the harlot, seated at the table in the barroom in San Francisco's Barbary Coast and placing a silver dollar on the tabletop near his empty glass. Presently the hulking vulgarian approached, the harlot took the silver dollar, and the samurai grimaced slightly at the foul body odor of the miner. "I ast what'cha sittin' with this li'l monkey fer," he blared. "Now I'm gonna skin 'is ass like a jackrabbit."

"A truly courageous man might let himself be cut before cutting someone else," the samurai had often declared. Indeed, Katsu lived by his words. One night in Kyoto, during the bloody reign of terror when men of the Shogunate were being assassinated one after the other under the pretense of "*Heaven's Revenge*," the navy commissioner walked through the dark streets escorted by a bodyguard. The bodyguard was a man of the Tosa clan by the name of Okada Izo, one of the most notorious killers of his time.

"Izo," Katsu said, "how many men have you killed?" Before Izo could reply, there was a thrashing sound of someone running straight at them.

"*Heaven's Revenge!*" a voice screamed in the darkness.

Izo drew his sword. Blue light flashed off his blade, followed by the screech of steel cutting through bone. He wiped the blood from his sword, then slid the blade back into his sheath. "Let's go, *Sensei*," he said calmly, as if he had not just killed a man. Katsu followed his bodyguard. He was terribly disturbed by the event he had just witnessed, all the more so because Izo seemed to have enjoyed it. "Izo," Katsu said, "you seem to get a thrill out of killing."

Izo offered no reply.

"Depending on the circumstances," Katsu admonished, "a truly courageous man might let himself be cut before cutting someone else."

"I don't understand," Izo said.

Nor did the hulking vulgarian, who now reached for his bowie knife, as the harlot drew the derringer from her buxom breast, and the samurai repeated calmly, "Another beer, please."

"Is that all you can say?" the harlot, slightly annoyed, asked the samurai, who, in truth, could say little more in English. She wondered whether the diminutive Oriental gentleman spoke from dense temerity or courageous indifference. The answer would have been apparent had she known that despite the very real danger to his life some eight years later, Katsu would choose not to keep a bodyguard at his home in Edo. Rather, he employed two or three maids, because, "*I assumed that even the most violent of men would never lay a hand on a woman.*"

"Very well," the harlot said, standing up. "I'll get you a beer."

"Later," the samurai now managed to articulate, and, as the harlot resumed her seat at the table, he motioned for the hulking vulgarian to sit down. Perhaps it was the strange dress of the samurai; or perhaps it was his calm and noble mien; or perhaps the imposing swords he wore at his left hip; or perhaps it was the look in Katsu's dark eyes which now subdued the much larger man, so that he uttered a profanity, scratched his thick red beard, shook his head and snorted twice loudly in vain protest, before yielding to the samurai's will.

Fidelity

Settings

A place just outside one of the Nine Forbidden Gates of the Imperial Palace in Kyoto, May 1863

Office of the police commissioner in Kyoto, May 1863

Players

Anenokoji Kintomo (*L*): A leader of radicals at the Imperial Court, who was mysteriously assassinated

Tanaka Shimbe (*L*): A Satsuma samurai, and notorious assassin in Kyoto

Fidelity

Fidelity was an intrinsic element of the code of the warrior, the essence of which was directed at the twofold sovereignty of liege lord and feudal clan. While samurai throughout Japan had historically demonstrated with their very lives loyalty to master and fellow clansmen, the warriors of the Satsuma clan were perhaps unsurpassed in the purity of the fidelity they embraced. It is no wonder, then, that Satsuma produced some of the most stoic warriors in Japan, with a readiness to die in the service of their lord preeminent.

On the moonless night of May 20, 1863, Anenokoji Kintomo, a radical leader at the Kyoto Court and champion of anti-Tokugawa *Imperial Loyalism*, was attacked and mortally wounded just outside Sakuhei Gate, one of Nine Forbidden Gates of the Imperial Palace.

The young court noble had been walking from the palace to his nearby home. The way was dark, the only light from a single lantern carried by one of five attendants. The first assailant was upon Anenokoji all of a sudden, cutting him about the side of the face before disappearing into the darkness. Four of the attendants fled, and one chased after the first assailant, while their master's blood gushed from his face. Another assailant now came from behind, thrusting his sword deeply into Anenokoji's back. A third assailant sliced open his chest. Wheezing in pain because he was unable to scream, the young noble fell to the ground. Aided by an attendant who had now returned to the scene, Anenokoji staggered a quarter of a mile toward his home, before collapsing along the way. This leader of the movement to expel the foreigners from Japan and overthrow the Shogunate was dead at age twenty-five.

Anenokoji was assassinated after a heated discussion with fellow officials of the Imperial Court, whose overwhelming consensus had been to issue an Imperial decree to the Choshu clan to topple the Bakufu. Choshu, one of the most powerful feudal domains in Japan and the darling of the radical court nobles, stood at the Loyalists' vanguard — their slogan: *Imperial Reverence and Expelling the Barbarians*.

On the day of the assassination it was reported to the Imperial Court that earlier in the month the Bakufu had paid Great Britain an indemnity in the enormous sum of four hundred thousand dollars, as demanded by the British government for the brutal killing of the Englishman Charles Lenox Richardson by Satsuma samurai during the previous August. Just two days before the indemnity had been paid, the Imperial Court had ordered the Bakufu to refuse Britain's demands. Anenokoji and his colleagues were outraged upon hearing that Edo had yielded to the British, bolstered though they were by an intimidating fleet, including nine heavily armed warships, moored in the harbor at Yokohama. The court now used the Bakufu's violation of an Imperial order as an excuse to issue a decree to the Lord of Choshu to rally his forces to crush the Tokugawa.

For fourteen generations the Shogun had ruled the Japanese nation, unopposed by the 260 *daimyo*. But opposition to the commercial treaties with foreign nations had so intensified that Shogun Tokugawa Iemochi had been compelled to pay a visit to Kyoto in March to guarantee the Emperor that the foreigners would be expelled by the tenth of May. This first visit to Kyoto by a Shogun in over two centuries, and the impossible promise he had made, aroused widespread doubt as to the Bakufu's ability to continue ruling the nation.

Choshu quickly seized this opportunity to increase its status among the xenophobic court nobles and to further diminish Bakufu prestige. On May eleventh, the renegade clan fired upon an American merchant ship as it passed through Shimonoseki Strait, at the southwestern point of the Choshu domain. On May twenty-third, a French dispatch-boat crossing the same waters was also attacked by Choshu. Three days later a Dutch corvette sailing from Nagasaki to Yokohama became the third target of Choshu guns at Shimonoseki.

The leaders of the movement for *Toppling the Bakufu and Imperial Loyalism* were men of Satsuma, Tosa and Choshu, three of the most powerful samurai clans. Only the Choshu men, however, enjoyed the support of their *daimyo*, and so an official mandate to openly oppose the Tokugawa. Choshu's blatant display of anti-Tokugawa sentiment and its official xenophobia naturally endeared that clan to the radicals at the Imperial Court, who were led by two young nobles, one of them Anenokoji.

Opposing *Toppling the Bakufu and Imperial Loyalism* were two other policies at the forefront of national politics. *Opening the Country and Support for the Bakufu* advocated free trade with foreign nations. A *Union of Court and Camp* called for an alliance between the Imperial Court at Kyoto and the military regime at Edo, to rally unity throughout Japan. To secure the union, Shogun Iemochi, age seventeen, would be married to the Emperor's sister, Princess Kazu, who was just two weeks older than the Shogun. Through this alliance the Bakufu would subdue the Loyalists, while Emperor Komei would be relieved, for the time being, of his fear of foreign subjugation, exacerbated by his ignorance of things Western and a chronic xenophobia. More than anything else, the Emperor desired national unity so that Japan might be strong enough to defend itself against the foreigners. He secretly detested the extremists who claimed to revere him, but who actually wreaked havoc throughout his capital.

Anenokoji's assailants had escaped into the darkness of the moonless night, their identity unknown. The shady circumstances of the assassination shrouded the already blood-soaked stage of Kyoto in an eerie shadow of intrigue. Satsuma, among others, suspected that its arch-rival, Choshu, was behind the murder. Choshu blamed Satsuma, while others accused the Bakufu of eliminating its dangerous enemy at court.

Satsuma's suspicions of Choshu, who enjoyed in the person of Anenokoji its staunchest ally at court, would have seemed preposterous just one month before the assassination. In April, however, Anenokoji had spent some twenty days aboard a Tokugawa warship with Katsu Kaishu, the brilliant commissioner of the Shogun's navy and one of Japan's leading advocates of *Opening the Country*. Katsu had been accompanying Shogun Iemochi on an inspection tour of the military fortifications along the coast near Osaka and Kobe, in western Japan. Assailed by the anti-Tokugawa radicals as a traitor, Katsu argued that, rather than trying to expel the foreigners and risking a war it could not hope to win, Japan must first strengthen itself through foreign trade to avoid subjugation. It was well known that Katsu was a gifted rhetorician who had convinced some of the staunchest anti-Bakufu Loyalists to relinquish their xenophobic convictions. The most renowned among Katsu's followers was Sakamoto Ryoma, who had been the right-hand man of Takechi Hanpeita,* the leader of the Tosa Loyalists and confidant of Anenokoji. Satsuma's suspicion that Choshu had arranged Anenokoji's murder was founded on rumors that Anenokoji had also been recruited by Katsu into the Tokugawa camp.

As if to bolster Satsuma's suspicions of Choshu, the sword of a Satsuma samurai had been found at the scene of the murder. Outraged, Satsuma accused Choshu of having stolen the sword and planting it at the crime scene. Satsuma's claim was not unfounded. Satsuma had thus far been in charge of guarding the Imperial Palace, but Choshu would now use the uncertain evidence of Satsuma guilt to secure the dismissal of its rival's troops from the coveted guard duty.

---

*Takechi Zuizan's given name was Hanpeita. Zuizan was his pseudonym.

Choshu had ample reason for suspecting Satsuma of Anenokoji's assassination. In the previous spring, it had been rumored that Shimazu Hisamitsu, father of the nominal Satsuma *daimyo* and *de facto* lord of that clan, would lead an army into Kyoto to embrace the Emperor, declare war on the Bakufu, and rally support among samurai throughout Japan to overthrow the Tokugawa and restore the Emperor to power. As Choshu and Satsuma were bitter rivals, the Choshu Loyalists were suspicious of Lord Hisamitsu's true intentions. Never before in two-and-a-half centuries of Tokugawa rule had a *daimyo* escorted an army into the Imperial capital. Choshu suspected that Satsuma would embrace the Emperor at the exclusion of the rest of the feudal domains, and set up an Imperial government under its control.

Choshu's hate for Satsuma was intensified by the latter clan's support for a *Union of Court and Camp*. While Choshu would risk its very existence to expel the foreigners and overthrow the Tokugawa for the sake of the Imperial Court, Satsuma collaborated with the Aizu clan, whose *daimyo* was a close relative of the Shogun, to realize the detested union, and, as a result, strengthen its own position at court. In order to usurp undisputed leadership from Choshu as chief mediator between the Imperial Court and the Bakufu, the Lord of Satsuma eventually led his army into Kyoto in June 1862, to advocate a *Union of Court and Camp*. Having succeeded in winning Imperial approval for a union, and being appointed by the court to establish law and order in Kyoto, the calculating Satsuma *daimyo* was assigned to escort two Imperial envoys to Edo, who carried an Imperial order for the Shogun to report to Kyoto for consultations with the Emperor. In the face of the none-too-subtle threat of one thousand Satsuma troops, the Shogun agreed to the Imperial order, which was actually a proposal by Lord Hisamitsu.

Upon his return to Kyoto, Lord Hisamitsu found that Choshu had regained the Imperial grace which had been his before he had left. Backed by the Choshu extremists, the Imperial Court would no longer abide by Satsuma's middle-of-the-road policy of a *Union of Court and Camp*. Rather, the battle cry of *Toppling the Bakufu and Imperial Loyalism* resounded through the dangerous streets of Kyoto, reflecting the sentiments raging among the Choshu zealots who had now gathered in the Imperial capital.

Meanwhile, Satsuma was embroiled in the Richardson Affair. Great Britain was demanding indemnity, and the arrest and execution of the Satsuma men who had murdered the Englishman, putting Satsuma in a very dangerous predicament. Great Britain threatened military retaliation upon the Satsuma domain unless its demands were met. Satsuma was not about to lose face by cowering to British intimidation, although it knew that its forces would be no match against British warships. Satsuma expected, however, that Edo would pay the indemnity, and thus mollify the British threat. When the court issued the Imperial decree forbidding the Bakufu to do so, Lord Hisamitsu may certainly have entertained the notion of assassinating Anenokoji.

Suspicion of Bakufu involvement in Anenokoji's murder was absurd. Although elimination of the radical leader at court would also have served the best interest of the Shogun, the Bakufu could not risk the consequences of assassinating Anenokoji. If it were to have become known that the Bakufu, or an agent of the Edo regime, had orchestrated the murder of an advisor to the Emperor, not only would the Tokugawa earn the wrath of the Imperial Court, but also the disdain of the entire nation. This would further diminish trust for the Bakufu among samurai clans throughout Japan, not to mention its mandate to rule the empire.

*   *   *

While Satsuma and Choshu pointed the finger at each other, the fact remained that the sword of a Satsuma man, one Tanaka Shimbe, had been found at the scene of the crime. The sword was identified by the name of the Satsuma smith who had forged the blade, which was inscribed on the tang. It was known that Tanaka's favorite sword bore the same inscription. When it was discovered that the sword with this inscription was no longer in Tanaka's possession, an order for his arrest was issued.

Tanaka was a known assassin, but his confederates knew that he was innocent of this crime. The ruthlessness with which Tanaka wielded a drawn sword had been demonstrated in numerous assassinations of Tokugawa supporters in and around Kyoto. Anenokoji had been attacked by three men. The first assailant had cut Anenokoji without killing him. The second and third assailants each delivered lethal blows, but Anenokoji had been able to stagger a quarter of a mile before finally collapsing. People close to Tanaka knew that death would have been instantaneous had Anenokoji's assassination been the work of the notorious hit man. They also knew that an assassin of Tanaka's caliber would never have left his sword behind. Circumstantial evidence notwithstanding, the fact remained that Tanaka's sword was found at the scene of the crime. The Satsuma man was arrested by Bakufu authorities in Kyoto six days after the assassination.

The samurai of Satsuma were unsurpassed in their tendency to look down upon the commoners. Tanaka had been born a commoner. He was also one of the dread "Four Butchers" who over this past year had terrorized Kyoto in the name of *Toppling the Bakufu and Imperial Loyalism.* Although he was not savvy about the intricacies and intrigues of national affairs, shortly after his arrival to Kyoto he discovered that by cutting down supporters of the Tokugawa he could command the respect, however superficial, of the leaders of the revolution. That he had sought this respect was, in all probability, due to a deep-seated inferiority complex over his common lineage, and a bitter awareness that he was good for nothing in this world but cold-blooded murder. Tanaka's first taste of bloodshed had been in the summer of 1862. His victim was a retainer to a former chief Imperial advisor, who several years before had caused the execution of *Men of High Purpose* of the Loyalist camp. Tanaka butchered the Imperial samurai with a vengeance. His bloodied head was found three days later atop a bamboo stake which had been stuck in the mud along the Kamogawa river. The headless corpse was discovered in the nearby Takasegawa canal. The murdered man had only been cut once, his body split open diagonally from the back of the right shoulder to the left hip. Shortly after this first assassination, Tanaka was elevated to samurai status by the Satsuma clan.

Before his arrest, which he knew was imminent, Tanaka vowed to himself that no matter what might happen he would behave as a samurai. He would not inform the authorities that his sword had actually been stolen at a Kyoto brothel several days prior to the assassination. Nor would he try to save his own life by reporting that even before the murder he had told a friend of the theft. Rather, as he now sat facing his interrogators at the office of the police commissioner in Kyoto, a single train of thought occupied his mind: It is unbecoming of a samurai to argue with words. I can best serve my lord and my clan by displaying my innocence with my life. And what if they do believe that I killed Anenokoji? Had he not recently become a turncoat who would sell out to the foreigners? Perhaps I would have killed him anyway.

"Is this your sword?" one of his interrogators asked, holding the sword in his hand.

"I don't know. I can't see it very well from here," Tanaka said. "I need to have a closer look."

When the sword was handed him, Tanaka slowly drew the blade and examined it. "Yes, this is definitely my sword," he declared in a low, clear voice. "But," he added, now loudly, "I did not kill Anenokoji."

"If you didn't kill him, then who...?"

Before the interrogator could finish speaking, and to the dismay of the startled authorities, Tanaka thrust his sword into the left side of his own belly, slicing across to the right side, and in the same gust of mental strength, brought the blade to his neck, severing the carotid artery.

Although Anenokoji's assassins would never be positively identified, Tanaka's suicide was, for the time being, taken as an admission of guilt. Satsuma consequently fell from Imperial grace, as Choshu and the radicals at court now reigned supreme in the frenzied ancient capital of the Japanese Emperor.

"Heaven's Revenge"

Settings
Several places in and around the Imperial capital, the latter half of 1862

Drawing room at the home of Yoshida Toyo, regent to the Lord of Tosa, fall 1861

Players
Honma Seiichiro (*L*): A *ronin* from the province of Echigo

Yoshida Toyo (*U*): Regent to the Lord of Tosa, who was assassinated by Tosa Loyalists

Takechi Zuizan (*L*): A Tosa samurai, master swordsman, the revolutionary leader of the Tosa Loyalists, and mastermind of assassinations

Okada Izo (*L*): A Tosa samurai, and notorious assassin in Kyoto

"Heaven's Revenge"

An ambush in the dark. A mangled head skewered atop a bamboo stake along a timeless river. A headless corpse floating in the shallows of a bloodied canal. Aftermaths of a nightly war cry resounding through the Imperial capital, transforming its quaint and ancient streets into so many scenes of unprecedented carnage. "Heaven's Revenge" was the death sentence roared by the warriors of Master Zuizan, wreaking terror among enemies of Imperial Loyalism with cold, razor-sharp steel.

It was a rainy night in August 1862. "*Heaven's Revenge,*" a voice cut the silence of a dark and desolate street near the canal. Honma Seiichiro, a *ronin* from the province of Echigo, drew his sword. An ear-piercing guttural wail ensued, and Honma wheezed in pain. He collapsed, and now another man holding a lantern was upon him. As Honma felt his life gush from his body in hot, red spurts, the man extended his hand. Honma reached out, and in desperation attempted to pull himself up from the muddy street. Nausea surged as Honma faced still another assailant. A drawn sword came crashing down, and an instant later the front of Honma's skull was split open.

The assassins carried the body to the nearby Kamogawa river. Here they severed the head, and skewered it atop a bamboo stake, on which was hung a wooden placard denouncing the dead man. They claimed he had "misled the people with lies, and slandered the Satsuma, Choshu and Tosa clans with false charges." They did not write, however, that they had butchered him for being a braggart whose very existence was detrimental to the Loyalist movement, or that he had falsely claimed responsibility for the assassination of Yoshida Toyo, the powerful regent to the Lord of Tosa.

Yoshida was a brilliant scholar and capable administrator. He was a staunch advocate of a *Union of Court and Camp.* He was also the Tosa *daimyo*'s favorite vassal. When Yamanouchi

Yodo, Lord of Tosa, had been forced into retirement by the Bakufu dictator Ii Naosuke, it was only natural that Yoshida would be appointed to the powerful post of regent. With Lord Yodo in confinement at his villa in Edo, Regent Yoshida ruled the Tosa domain.

Yoshida clashed with Takechi Zuizan, master of the Zuizan Fencing Academy, stoic warrior, and leader of the Tosa Loyalists. The elitist regent had been Zuizan's greatest obstacle in uniting the Tosa clan behind the movement for *Toppling the Bakufu and Imperial Loyalism*. Zuizan's family was of the lower echelons of samurai society in Tosa. Regent Yoshida was born into the privileged upper-samurai classes.

For centuries the lower-samurai of Tosa had been suppressed by the upper-samurai. Dress codes existed so that the two classes could be easily distinguished. The lower-samurai were forbidden to wear wooden clogs, and, in certain instances, silk; and no matter how hot the weather, it was against the law for any but upper-samurai to carry a parasol to screen the sunlight when in close vicinity to the lord's castle. Occasionally this discrimination was carried to extremes. Men of the upper classes were permitted by law to strike down their social inferiors, but under no circumstances were lower-samurai allowed to draw their swords on upper-samurai.

That Yoshida refused to incorporate Zuizan's radical plans into government policy because of his low rank disturbed the Loyalist leader. That the regent would never take him seriously infuriated him. But the calculating Zuizan was not one to display his emotions, particularly to his enemies. He had over these past several years emerged as the undisputed leader of the hot-blooded young men of lower-samurai stock throughout the Tosa domain. At age thirty-three, the charismatic sword master had recently formed the Tosa Loyalist Party in Kochi. Nearly two hundred Tosa men had sealed in blood their party's manifesto, "for those men," Master Zuizan had declared, "who will fight to overthrow the Bakufu, expel the barbarians, and return the rule of the nation to His Imperial Majesty in Kyoto."

"*It is a source of deepest grief to our Emperor,*" the manifesto began, "*that our magnificent and divine country has been humiliated by the barbarians and that the Spirit of Japan, which has been transmitted from antiquity, is on the brink of being extinguished.*" The manifesto proclaimed that every member of the party must be willing to "*go through fire and water to ease the Emperor's mind...and to purge this evil from our people.*" Should any man put personal considerations before the Loyalist cause, "*he shall incur the punishment of the angered gods...and be summoned before his comrades to commit seppuku.*"

Zuizan had visited the regent's home in the previous fall. This was his last effort to convince Yoshida of the wisdom of his vision for a grand alliance between Tosa, Choshu and Satsuma, to rally their forces to overthrow the Shogunate and form a new Imperial government in Kyoto.

"Unless Tosa takes the appropriate measures," Zuizan had warned, as the two sat in the regent's drawing room, "we will fall behind Choshu and Satsuma." The sword master's severe, dark eyes complimented his pallid complexion and betrayed an unyielding will to power. "Choshu and Satsuma are going to unite to embrace the Emperor with thousands of troops at the Imperial Palace in Kyoto, and topple the Bakufu. Such a display of military strength will attract support among the other clans. We must not permit Tosa to be branded a traitor to the Emperor for not having officially endorsed *Imperial Loyalism.*"

Yoshida met Zuizan's piercing eyes with derisive laughter. "You haven't read enough Japanese history," the regent said condescendingly. "Throughout the ages, each time the Emperor and the court nobles have voiced their opinions, trouble has inevitably ensued. Whenever the court has tried to seize political power, there has always been a war. And now they are starting to make noise again in Kyoto. Certainly you know that it was the founders of the three military governments throughout Japanese history who were successful in bringing peace to our nation. Use your head! Give up your sophomoric ideas. A man of your intelligence and influence should be of service to Tosa, not a negative force working against us."

Yoshida Toyo supported the Bakufu's drive for a *Union of Court and Camp*. He looked upon the court nobles as incompetents who refused to consider the policies necessary to cope with the changing times. They needed to be controlled, he said. An alliance between Kyoto and Edo would provide a satisfactory means by which to dominate those whom Yoshida considered to be "the renegade Loyalists in Kyoto," and whom Zuizan would represent.

Zuizan suppressed his rage, collected his thoughts and began to speak in a cool, deliberate manner. "Yoshida-sensei, it is my every intention to be of service to Tosa. I therefore implore you to heed our manifesto." He thrust the document at his nemesis as if it were a weapon by which he would topple the conservative Tosa regime.

Yoshida ran his eyes over the blood-sealed manifesto, and sardonically laughed aloud. "You don't really believe that we can expel the barbarians without first opening up the country," he said. "First we must conduct trade with the barbarians in order to enrich ourselves to a degree that we can deal with them on our own terms. How do you expect to defeat the barbarians when we don't even have one decent warship of our own? You seem to be telling me that a band of lower-samurai have taken it upon themselves to join forces with the upper-samurai to reform Tosa policy. How could you," he now yelled angrily, "have the impudence to assume that I would even consider such a preposterous idea? It seems you are asking me to grant the lower-samurai the right to participate in the administration of the great domain of Tosa."

"Yes, for the good of Tosa and the Empire..."

"Over my dead body," Yoshida roared.

Zuizan's eyes flashed as a dark thought crossed his mind, and a momentary silence resounded through the regent's drawing room.

Yoshida Toyo was ambushed on a rainy night in the following April, just outside the main gain of Kochi Castle. His head was discovered the next morning along a nearby river.

Having eliminated his nemesis, Zuizan arranged for two Loyalist sympathizers from among the upper-samurai to be appointed Great Inspectors of the Tosa domain, which put them in charge of the police force. Master Zuizan's will, though masked it remained, now found its way deep into the nerve center of the Tosa government. The shrewd Loyalist Party leader delighted in his success at gaining control of the reins of power. As he basked in his newfound glory in Kochi, the retired *daimyo* raged at his villa in Edo, where he had been under forced confinement for most of these past three years. Yamanouchi Yodo, likened to a tiger by even the most powerful of feudal lords, was not about to sit back passively while a band of lower-samurai renegades assumed control of his own domain.

Master Zuizan left Kochi in June to further the Loyalists' cause in Kyoto. Adept in terrorist tactics, he would now wield his carefully chosen death squad to inflict *Heaven's Revenge* upon his enemies. He would rise to the forefront of Kyoto politics, and, through the auspices of two young radical nobles, gain influence over the Imperial Court.

Master Zuizan was a man of culture. He had distinguished himself as an expert in the way of the sword at a top fencing academy in Edo. An accomplished Confucian scholar, he was well-versed in the Chinese classics, and gifted in the arts of poetry, painting and calligraphy. He was also an intensely proud man who was painfully concerned with his own worth, and whose lust for power knew no bounds. Accustomed to assuming majestic airs to overwhelm, he used his superior rhetorical skill to dupe his less intellectual followers into obeying his every command. Most of his following in Kyoto consisted of

Tosa men who had studied at the Zuizan Fencing Academy in Kochi. His most adroit fencing student was an uneducated rustic by the name of Okada Izo. Izo was spellbound by the intellect of his master, whose depths he could not fathom. But Izo was a genius of a different calling — with an unsheathed sword in hand, his ability to kill was unmatched even by Master Zuizan himself.

Two days after Honma's murder, the head of another enemy of the rebels was found mounted atop a bamboo stake along the same river. The murdered man was a retainer to a former chief Imperial advisor who had worked under Ii Naosuke. Ii, the powerful Lord of Hikone and direct retainer of the Shogun, was the devil incarnate in the eyes of the *s*. Several years before, Ii had been appointed Tokugawa Regent. As regent, he had assumed dictatorial control of the Bakufu, committed *lese majesty* by authorizing commercial treaties with foreign nations without Imperial sanction, and unleashed his Great Purge of anti-Tokugawa Imperial Loyalists throughout Japan. For his crimes, Regent Ii was assassinated at the gates of Edo Castle two years after coming to power. Master Zuizan's most recent victim had assisted Regent Ii in the arrests and subsequent executions of *Men of High Purpose*, and in the plot to marry the Emperor's sister to the Shogun.

The sweltering last day of August witnessed a gathering of Loyalists at Master Zuizan's private quarters at an inn in the Kawaramachi district of Kyoto. These quarters served as a command post from which Zuizan devised his plans for *Heaven's Revenge* against Tokugawa supporters, former henchmen of Regent Ii, and other undesirable elements whom the Loyalist leader deemed "harmful to the nation."

"We must get him today," Zuizan said calmly, stroking his long chin.

"Please let me kill him, *Sensei*," a man implored.

"*Heaven's Revenge*," cried Izo with religious fervor. "I want to do it." Sweat ran down the sides of Izo's sunbaked face, his mouth slightly open, his front teeth protruding.

"I want to kill him," said another man.

"So do I," implored several others.

"There are too many of you who want to cut him,' Zuizan said. "You'll have to draw lots."

"*Sensei*," said another man, "we shouldn't dirty our swords on a filthy animal like that. We should strangle him instead."

The "filthy animal" was more specifically known as the "Kyoto Monkey." His greatest crime had been to serve as a lackey to the recently murdered Imperial retainer, earning reward money for his part in the arrests of Loyalists eventually executed by Regent Ii. He had also snuck into the Imperial Palace and violated a lady of the court. Although rape was a capital crime, execution would have scandalized the lady and defiled the Imperial Court. Instead, a red-hot branding iron was taken to his face, for the immediate physical torture and the lasting disgrace. The Kyoto Monkey had recently purchased a brothel in order to divulge information from customers regarding the assassination of his master during the previous month. The brothel was to be opened for business on the following day.

Okada Izo and two others were selected to carry out the assassination of the Kyoto Monkey. That night they broke into his house and captured him alive. They took him to a deserted place along the river, near the Sanjo Bridge. Here they tortured him until he divulged the names of Bakufu police agents in Kyoto who had arrested *Men of High Purpose*, and of court nobles who advocated a *Union of Court and Camp*. Next they strangled him with a piece of rope, and to add ignominy to misery, they stripped the dead body for public view, and tied it spread-eagle to two wooden posts driven deep into the mud near the timeless river.

Master Zuizan was relentless. On the morning of September twenty-third, twenty-five Loyalists left Kyoto under a leaden sky. They traveled eastward on foot along the Tokaido Road. They had divided into several small groups to avoid attracting attention to themselves and their radical plan: the assassination of four Tokugawa police agents responsible for the arrests and executions of *Men of High Purpose* three years before. Their identity had been made known to the Loyalists by the Kyoto Monkey, as he was tortured along the river some three weeks earlier. Takechi Zuizan had been informed just two days ago that the four Bakufu men would return to Edo this very morning. He and Loyalist leaders of the Satsuma, Choshu and Kurume clans wasted no time in organizing a hit squad of twenty-five men.

That evening the Bakufu men stopped at an outpost town along the way. They took rooms at an inn, where they had intended to spend the night. When twenty-five masked men wearing white war headbands, their drawn swords in hand, burst into their rooms, the Bakufu men were taken completely off guard. Three of them were decapitated on the spot. The fourth man was mortally cut as he escaped into the darkness, though his bloody corpse was not found until the next morning. The heads of the three decapitated men were mounted that night atop bamboo stakes to publicize their crimes.

On the night of November fourteenth, the forty-five-year-old mistress of the late confidant of Regent Ii was abducted from her home. Her assailants dragged her by the hair through the streets to the Sanjo Bridge, where they pilloried her to the pilings for public view. Although her life was spared because she was a women, her son was captured the following night. Also dragged through the streets, he was blindfolded, forced to lean over a roadside gutter and methodically beheaded. The head was hung by the hair to the branch of a tree for public display. While the woman's punishment was intended as a public warning of the dangers of sympathizing with the Bakufu, the man's only crime was that he had been born his mother's son.

Heaven's Revenge would continue to resound through the

streets of the Imperial capital until 1864. During the three years that assassins would terrorize Kyoto, more than one hundred people would die at their hands. Takechi Zuizan, however, did not remain in Kyoto to witness the glory of his bloody legacy. In October he served as personal bodyguard to two Imperial envoys dispatched by the court to Edo to demand that the Bakufu renounce its foreign treaties and resume its centuries-old policy of seclusionism. Upon a brief return to the Imperial capital, he was appointed to the important post of director of Tosa headquarters in Kyoto, and granted the rank of upper-samurai. In the following spring, however, Master Zuizan received orders to return to his native Kochi, where he would tragically challenge the iron will of the Lord of Tosa.

The Remnants of
Shock

Settings

Verandah overlooking the garden of a venerable old house in Kochi, former castletown of the Lord of Tosa, spring 1890

Kochi Castletown in the 1860s

Ruins of a house in Tokyo, August 1945

Players

Hirose Kenta (*L*): A Tosa samurai forced to commit *seppuku*

Hirai Shujiro (*L*): A Tosa samurai forced to commit *seppuku*

Masaki Tetsuma (*L*): A Tosa samurai forced to commit *seppuku*

Yamanouchi Yodo (*L*): Lord of Tosa

The Remnants of Shock

To the samurai, seppuku epitomized a courageous life through a stoic and noble death. Self-disembowelment was not only an agonizing form of suicide, but an opportunity for the samurai to display his inner purity by exposing his bowels, the seat of his courage. It was often a legal form of punishment through which the condemned man could avoid the ignominy of execution. It was a vehicle of apology, and a means of absolution for the miscreant to prove his sincerity and redeem honor for himself, his family, his clan and his liege lord.

Traditionally, the function of the samurai was to accomplish deeds of valor at the risk of his own life. Accordingly, to be well-versed in the formal practice of seppuku was part of the samurai's basic education. As far as circumstances allowed,* seppuku was performed with the ceremony of a highly developed art form. Even with a razor-sharp blade, however, it can be difficult to cut through the human abdomen; the tissue is resilient and tends to have a springing effect against the tip of a sword. Accordingly, seppuku demanded of its practitioner absolute composure in the face of excruciating pain, an unfathomable resolve to plunge in the blade, and the will power to cut properly.

The practitioner was most often assisted by a second, in the person of a trusted friend, disciple or relative. The role of the second was every bit as important as that of the practitioner, and probably more technically difficult. The second had to be an accomplished swordsman who, ideally, would only brandish his sword after the practitioner had duly sliced open his abdomen. His task of decapitation demanded unflinching accuracy, impeccable timing and undaunted strength of mind. He had to be certain to strike exactly with the cutting edge, at which

---

*A man wounded in battle and facing imminent capture would not have the luxury of ceremony in committing *seppuku.*

instant he would pull hard on the blade to cut through tough sinews and bone, and sever the head of a person he cherished. The purpose of the second was twofold — to minimize the misery of the practitioner, and to assist him in accomplishing a beautiful death. Unless performed with perfect precision, self-disembowelment without a second could be a long, harrowing ordeal, accompanied by a shameful and sickening scene of protruding intestines. And just as the second assisted the practitioner, the favor was reciprocated. After cutting open his abdomen, the practitioner was obligated to fall forward, his arms extended before him, to facilitate his second's task. Falling backward or to either side would make decapitation difficult, if not impossible. It might cause the second the humiliation of missing his target altogether, or striking the practitioner on the head, or in more extreme cases, shoulder, back or elsewhere. And the torrent of blood had to be aimed in the proper direction, or, as the case may be, into a blood vat in front of the headless corpse, so as not to cause an unsightly mess, or cover the second or witnesses with the gore.

The year was 1890. The old man's heart still bore the remnants of shock from the horrendous task of nearly three decades past which it had been his honorable yet unhappy lot to inherit. And telltale of the traumatic effect of this shock, its remnants occasionally manifested themselves as a sudden and furious twitch on his sexagenarian face. In his youth he had been a samurai of the Tosa clan, and a member of the Tosa Loyalist Party. I only had the pleasure of meeting him once, at his ancestral home in Kochi, the former castletown of the Lord of Tosa, which, of course, is the capital of the modern prefecture of the same name. I made the long, exhausting journey from Tokyo to this most remote outback on the island of Shikoku, to interview the old man, one of the last surviving relics of the Tosa Loyalists of the 1860s. I was then employed as the Tokyo correspondent of a great American newspaper, whose name I shall not divulge in these pages, because, during that time I had grown weary of my journalistic occupation, and was consumed with writing a book about the troubled and bloody years leading up to the fall of the Tokugawa Shogunate. I had been informed by a colleague in the Japanese press that the old man was a living treasure chest of insight into the awe-inspiring legacy of his comrades in the revolution, and their heroic though horrible deaths.

The old house — one of many stately samurai residences which had lined the streets of the castletown for centuries — was a dark wooden, two-storied structure with white plastered sides, its garden bounded by similarly plastered walls. The roof of the house and the tops of the walls were of black tiles, which glistened in the bright sunlight and called to mind, as I passed through the wooden gate, that two and a half centuries of feudalism had only ended in this country twenty-odd years before. "Welcome," the old man greeted me at the front door, and, to my relief, with a cordial smile. This was the first time, I believe, that he had ever received a foreign guest into his home. But I had been duly introduced by my above-mentioned colleague, whose father had known the old man in their youth. My good colleague had written the old man a letter advising him of my fluency in the Japanese language, and the purpose of my visit.

The old man was dressed in a kimono of dark brown silk, and I felt suddenly self-conscious of my suit and tie, as if the Western dress was somehow intrusive amidst these surroundings of old Japan. His eyes, which I imagined were once flashing dark orbs of hot-blooded youth, had mellowed into watery pools of memories made poignant over years of tranquillity, but scarred, nevertheless, with that sudden and furious twitch. It was a balmy spring afternoon, conducive to tales of the romantic valor of yesteryear, heard outdoors over a cup of hot tea, on the verandah overlooking the garden of the venerable old home of the Masaki family. But the horrible tales which the old man imparted to me, authenticated by his twitch, would have been more aptly related in the grim dead of winter.

*   *   *

"It was the golden age of the Tosa Loyalists in Kyoto," the old man began speaking in the melodic Tosa dialect, which at once suggested the mild Kochi climate and the rich bounty of its earth and sea. "Takechi-sensei had arranged the assassination of Yoshida Toyo in April 1862. In the summer of the same year, he unofficially united Tosa behind *Toppling the Bakufu and Imperial Loyalism.* This meant, of course, that, for all intents and purposes, he was in control of the Tosa government. I suppose they were overstepping their bounds, Takechi-sensei and his men, because after they arrived in Kyoto that summer, they started to meddle in the affairs of the Imperial Court.

"Satsuma and Choshu had already stationed troops in Kyoto. Of course, Takechi-sensei wanted to have our own troops stationed there as well. He said that Tosa must join forces with Satsuma and Choshu in the revolution. He feared that otherwise we would be left behind after the Tokugawa had been overthrown, and the Imperial Court restored to power, and that all of the glory would go to Satsuma and Choshu. Of course, Takechi-sensei was right, and that's what eventually did happen. But most of us refused to accept one simple fact," the old man paused slightly, displaying only now a deep-seated animosity toward Yamanouchi Yodo, the late former *daimyo* of Tosa, the accomplished swordsman, the "poet warrior," the notorious imbiber, the self-styled Drunken Lord of the Sea of Whales, one of Four Brilliant Lords of his time, and the brazen egoist whose wrath, once incited, knew no bounds. "And that fact was that Lord Yodo would never side against the Tokugawa." Yodo owed his very position as Lord of Tosa to the Tokugawa, the old man explained. Before the Tokugawa had come to power, Tosa had been under the rule of the House of Chosokabe. When the warlord who would be the first Tokugawa Shogun defeated his enemies at the decisive Battle of Sekigahara at the turn of the seventeenth century, he confiscated the lands of the Chosokabe, who had sided against him, and awarded them to a minor feudal lord, the head of the House of Yamanouchi, who, although not a direct Tokugawa retainer, had not opposed him. "And it was for this reason, and one other which I shall explain momentarily, that Lord Yodo ordered my cousin and two other leaders of the Tosa Loyalist Party to commit *seppuku*. It was cowardly and unjust of Lord Yodo. Those three men did not deserve to die. They only had in mind the best interest of Tosa and the House of Yamanouchi when they asked the Imperial prince to write that letter urging Tosa to lend its official support to *Toppling the Bakufu and Imperial Loyalism*. Ostensibly they were sentenced to die for the 'crime of deceit.' Of course, that was sheer nonsense. The real reasons they were sentenced to death were because of their anti-Bakufu convictions, and Lord Yodo's fury over their audacity. He said they had overstepped their bounds by meddling in Tosa affairs after the assassination of Yoshida Toyo, then behind his back at the Imperial Court. Takechi-sensei pleaded with him to spare their lives, citing their loyalty to the *daimyo* and to the great domain of Tosa. But," the old man paused, his right eye twitching, "Lord Yodo just wouldn't listen."

Lord Yodo was indeed furious with his errant vassals, who over that past year had usurped the political power of his own domain. He advocated a *Union of Court and Camp*, and staunchly opposed the call to arms against the Tokugawa. Having recently emerged from a three-year bout of political paralysis at his villa in Edo, the strong-willed Lord of Tosa would now crush the Tosa Loyalists. The first three victims of his wrath were Masaki Tetsuma, Hirai Shujiro, and Hirose Kenta, all lieutenants to party leader Takechi Hanpeita. In the spring of 1863 they were arrested in Kyoto and returned immediately to Kochi, where they were thrown in jail. Shortly after, the three were sentenced to commit *seppuku*.

Hirose Kenta had studied the proper way to perform *seppuku*, because, as the old man now explained in an effluent burst of emotional pride, "in Tosa, a man's value was determined by how well he could cut himself."

"I see," I said not a little bit inanely, because, I suppose, I was much taken aback.

"Yes. Hirose was a tough man. But I did not have the honor of witnessing his *seppuku*."

The old man nevertheless recounted in meticulous detail that Hirose had been dressed in ceremonial white. That he had calmly kneeled down upon a clean tatami mat, and asked his second not to draw his sword until he had completed his final task. That under the steely gaze of the official inspector, Hirose had taken up the unsheathed dagger from a small untreated wooden stand, had glanced briefly at his second, then, without further hesitation, had plunged the dagger into the left side of his belly. "He immediately sliced across to his right side," the old man said, drawing an imaginary dagger across his own abdomen. "Then after cutting diagonally upward with the tip of the blade, he stabbed himself through the heart." The old man paused, released a heavy sigh, then sipped tea from a ceramic cup. "So perfectly did he cut, and with such firm resolve, that his second could offer no assistance."

The old man's voice dropped momentarily, then he said in a sudden spurt, "Hirai Shujiro carved his death poem with his fingernails on the walls of his cell. When he kneeled down to perform his *seppuku*, he noticed that his second was pale and extremely tense. 'Relax,' he told him, then loosened the sash of his white kimono, and rubbed his hand over the portion of his belly he would cut. He took the bare dagger from the stand in front of him, and plunged it into his lower abdomen. The second drew his sword, and immediately thrust it into Hirai's side. 'Again,' Hirai screamed, his face contorted in agony. An instant later the second delivered another blow, putting Hirai out of his misery.

74

"Masaki Tetsuma was an accomplished poet and brilliant scholar of the Chinese classics. He had been a child prodigy, who at the age of twenty had his own private academy in Kochi. They wouldn't give my cousin a calligraphy brush in his cell, so he composed his death poem with strips of paper that he had wound into pieces of thin chord. In his poem, he expressed his pleasure that the Imperial Court had regained political power. But he bitterly regretted that the Tosa banner would not fly in the Imperial capital alongside those of Choshu and Satsuma. I'll never forget it," the old man now paused, turning suddenly away, as if to hide the tears that I supposed had welled up in his eyes. "They wouldn't give him a calligraphy brush, but they gave him lots of *sake*. I think he was quite drunk when he kneeled down to perform his *seppuku*. Ah, you should have heard him denounce Lord Yodo for his indecisiveness in the face of the Bakufu. It was such a pleasure. But then he started to weep. The tears streamed down his face. That dark complexion, the pointed chin, and those penetrating eyes of his. He could look right through you with those eyes. And he was a big man, well over six feet tall. But he couldn't cut himself. They said he was a coward who just didn't have it in him."

"A coward?" I gasped, unable to control myself. "I can't believe..."

"Of course he wasn't a coward," the old man interrupted. "My cousin was a samurai through and through. But he was so overcome with indignation at the injustice of the three of them having been sentenced to die, although they had only acted for the good of Tosa, that he simply froze up. Maybe it was because of all the *sake* he had drank, but he was unable to take firm hold of the dagger. He looked up at me. He told me with his eyes what I must do." The old man paused, before taking a deep breath. "Then I drew my sword and beheaded him. He was only twenty-nine years old."

I left the old man and his ancestral home in Kochi shortly after. As I bid him farewell, on the verandah overlooking the garden on that balmy spring day three decades ago, I felt suddenly laden with an inexplicable funereal despair. I dismissed it as an inevitable consequence of the grim accounts I had just heard, and went about my way. But a fortnight later, when I received a telegram at my office in Tokyo informing me of the old man's passing, I could not help but feel that somehow, someway, and for reasons I would never understand, I had had a premonition of the imminent demise of that living relic of the age of the samurai.

*   *   *

Modernization is a powerful force. Technological innovation follows in its wake. Society changes, but culture spanning centuries does not disappear. Nor did the practice of seppuku, nor the code of the warrior, vanish with the age of the samurai.

A scene comes to mind — as pathetic as horrible, yet somehow noble, even heroic. It is early morning in Tokyo, in late August 1945. The Emperor has just announced to the people Japan's defeat in the war. The landing in Tokyo of the Allied Forces is imminent. The Japanese capital is a desolate field of ashes. Protruding here and there are skeleton frames of burnt out buildings, massacred like their hundreds of thousands of human occupants. A young girl awakes from a vivid nightmare of foreign troops storming her house, and violating her in unspeakable ways. She has been sleeping alone in the ruins of what was once the kitchen of her family's home. She has ample reason to be filled with dread at the impending landing of the enemy forces. She has been taught by her parents and school teachers that the American and British soldiers are devils, who would rape the women and castrate the men. Yesterday she cut off her long black hair to pass for a boy, but she knew her attempt was futile.

There is a loud explosion in the distance. But after the horror of months of fire bombing the young girl no longer trembles.

She is left only with the remnants of shock, and a stoic will to control her own destiny. She has not yet gotten dressed, but fearing that she has no time to waste, reaches for the table knife she has kept handy for such an emergency. The blade is thick and dull, the handle short, but this is the only knife she has. She wets a towel in a small pail of water, and wraps it around the handle so that the blood will not cause her to lose her grip. She does not know the proper way to cut, nor does she have a second to assist her, but is nevertheless determined to preserve her dignity. She kneels down on the cement floor, which is covered with ashes and soot. She recites a short Buddhist prayer, and with the resolve of her ancestors, plunges the knife into her lower abdomen. Blood gushes from the wound, pain grips her, but she pulls the knife out, and repeats the process, once, twice, then a third time. She falls over on her side, blood trickles from her mouth, but death does not yet come. She languishes utterly alone, unable to move, as the morning turns into afternoon. The heat is stifling, flies hover about, a teardrop runs down the side of her cheek and onto the floor of her mother's kitchen, until happily, triumphant in her honor, the young girl dies.

"A Truly
Despicable World"

Settings

A jail cell in Kochi Castletown, July 1864

Courthouse garden near the jail, May 1865

Players

Takechi Zuizan (*L*): A Tosa samurai, master swordsman, and the revolutionary leader of the Tosa Loyalists

Yamanouchi Yodo (*L*): Lord of Tosa

"A Truly Despicable World"

That Takechi Zuizan was the founder of an outlawed revolutionary party, a meticulous planner of cold-blooded murder, a master manipulator of admirers and enemies alike, a weaver of terror in the hearts of men who was excessively concerned with his own worth are historical facts. From these facts arises a question: Was Master Zuizan a megalomaniac? After close scrutiny, let us venture the opinion that he was not. Rather, we should say that he suffered from delusions of grandeur, and that these delusions were the genesis of his overwhelming will to power, wherein lay his greatness and the seed of his ultimate destruction.

Lord Yodo had recently been released from nearly three years of forced confinement at his villa in Edo. The strong willed *daimyo* would now crush the renegade Tosa Loyalist Party, which during the term of his confinement had transformed into a monster, threatening his rule over Tosa. Lord Yodo knew that to crush the Loyalists, he must destroy their leader. As long as Takechi Zuizan was alive, the danger of rebellion throughout the seven districts of Tosa remained very real. To regain complete control of his domain, he must sever the head of the rebellious monster.

But Lord Yodo had another, even darker reason to eliminate Master Zuizan. Since returning from Kyoto to Kochi Castletown in the spring of 1863, Zuizan had very brazenly attempted to convince the *daimyo* to abandon his duty to the Tokugawa and unite Tosa behind *Imperial Loyalism*. Upon one occasion, he had even dared utter to Yodo, "My Lord, to dwell so fervently on the favor your august ancestors received from the Tokugawa two and a half centuries ago, particularly now when the very future of Japan is at stake, could be likened to the idle fancy of a fool." It was this outrage that Lord Yodo would never forgive.

But Master Zuizan's lust for power had grown so intense, his ego so enormous, that he refused to believe Lord Yodo would not see things his way, insisting to himself and his followers that the Tosa *daimyo* secretly embraced *Imperial Loyalism*.

Master Zuizan was tragically mistaken. He was arrested in Kochi in September 1863. On the morning of his arrest, he had risen at dawn, as was his custom. He washed his face in a basin of cool well water, donned his riding clothes — black pleated trousers, a black jacket and a short-rimmed military helmet — then told his wife that he was going for a ride. When he returned to his home an hour later, he found one of his men waiting in the front garden.

The police were after him, the man informed hastily. He entreated the Loyalist leader to flee Tosa immediately in order to avoid arrest. Master Zuizan would hear nothing of it. Even now he refused to believe that the Lord of Tosa would not abide by his will. He was convinced that Lord Yodo's support for a *Union of Court and Camp* was mere ostentation, designed to appease the authorities in Edo. While it was true that Zuizan had ordered the assassination of the lord's regent, the murder was unavoidable if he was to unite Tosa under *Imperial Loyalism*. And certainly, Master Zuizan believed, Lord Yodo would eventually embrace his noble cause.

*   *   *

The afternoon of July 14, 1864 was exceptionally hot in the southern climes of Kochi Castletown. Zuizan sat alone in his jail cell, staring at his own reflection in the dim, still water of a small basin. The body was emaciated, the cheeks hollow, the bearded face haggard and the long black hair tattered after nearly a year of languishing in jail. But from the eyes, set in deep dark sockets of disgust at the world and the petty ways of men, radiated a spiritual strength unknown to the likes of all but a select few. Zuizan picked up a brush which his wife had sent him, along with ink, paper and other implements of his art. He began painting his own image, not as it appeared in the dim basin, but as he painfully perceived it in the clarity of his mind's eye. Zuizan completed his self-portrait and sent it to his wife, along with the words "if I should die, keep this in the house" as a remembrance, because he now felt certain that death was near.

Although the bitter cold of the previous winter had made him ill, summer was the most unbearable time of year to be locked up. The wooden floor of his cell afforded barely enough space for him to lie down; and although his wife sent his favorite foods to him daily, often he was unable to eat for the sickening stench of the latrine intensified by the stifling heat. Not even in sleep could he find relief, for the jail was infested with rats, mosquitoes, lice and ticks.

The interrogation had started in the previous May. Lord Yodo had ordered the chief interrogators, both former devoted followers of Yoshida Toyo, to uncover evidence linking Zuizan to the regent's assassination. After a year of interrogation, Zuizan wrote in a letter to his wife, *"They don't listen to a thing I say, but rather continue to insist that I'm guilty."* Summing up his feelings, he lamented, *"Ah, what a truly despicable world this is."*

The interrogation and investigation lasted for over a year and a half, but Yodo's men were still unable to find conclusive evidence of Zuizan's guilt. Lord Yodo was at his wit's end, and on the morning of intercalary May fifteenth, having concluded that "impudence toward the *daimyo*" was sufficient reason for his indomitable vassal to die, issued an order for Zuizan to commit *seppuku*. When Zuizan was informed soon after that he must die that very evening, he was overcome, however briefly, with tears of joy. Since his arrest, his greatest fear had been that he might be put to the ignominy of the executioner's sword. Of this he would now be spared, and permitted to die as honorably as he had lived. And though his body was sick and depleted of its once formidable strength, he was determined to die as a samurai. He would achieve beauty in death, the culmination of a life given to practice in the way of the sword and the noble code of the warrior.

In preparation for his *seppuku*, Zuizan bathed, because, as he told his guards, "it would be unsightly to have dirt on the dead body." Next he shaved his face and pate, oiled and combed his hair, and tied his topknot. He dressed himself in special attire sent him by his wife: a thin kimono of pale blue hempen cloth adorned with the Takechi family crest, and a stiff ceremonial robe bound by a silken sash. Thus prepared, he returned to his dark, dank cell to wait to be called upon to die.

At dusk he was brought to the nearby courthouse garden, where he had been interrogated in the past. The scene this evening, however, was different from that which he had known. The ground was specially covered with sand to absorb Zuizan's blood. Several men in formal dress were seated in a semicircle, facing an area on the north side of the garden furnished with two tatami mats. Two candles burning in two tall stands cast a dim pallor over the grim scene, and Zuizan recognized among the witnesses the two chief interrogators. Suppressing a sudden desire to throw himself upon them, he calmly seated himself upon the tatami.

Set directly in front of him was an untreated, pale wooden stand, on top of which had been placed a piece of clean white cotton cloth and a dagger in a plain wooden sheath. Earlier in the day he had chosen his two seconds, both former *kenjutsu* students and adept swordsmen, who now sat at either side of him. One of them was the younger brother of his wife, the other Zuizan's nephew. One of the chief interrogators now read in a loud clear voice the death sentence, after which Master Zuizan bowed deeply. "Thank you for your troubles," he said to his seconds, taking the dagger in his hand and drawing the blade.

Master Zuizan would now perform his *seppuku* with meticulous precision. He believed that there were only three proper ways to cut — one straight horizontal line, two intersecting lines, or three horizontal lines. He chose the latter, which was the least common, because it was the most difficult to perform properly. But so weak was his physical condition after one and a half years in jail, that it had been a struggle for him to even walk to the courthouse garden. Over these past several days he had continuously suffered from chronic diarrhea, abdominal pain, fever, and a palsy that numbed his entire body. He worried that he would not have the physical strength to slice through the resilient abdominal tissue three separate times. He feared that if he should fail to perform his *seppuku* beautifully his name would be slandered in death, and his enemies would laugh and call him a coward who was unable to die like a samurai. He had therefore informed one of his guards of the cutting method he had chosen, making him swear to publicize his noble intent in the case that his physical strength should fail him.

"Don't cut me until I give the command," he told his seconds. He stared hard at the blade, then gently replaced the dagger on the stand. He cast a steely gaze at the several witnesses, who, in spite of their exalted positions, were daunted by the superior strength radiating from the eyes of the man with the emaciated body. Master Zuizan now removed both arms from his kimono, baring his pale shoulders, then loosened the sash around his waist, exposing his lower abdomen. He tightened his mind as he summoned all of his mental power into his hands, again took up the bare dagger, wrapped the hilt with the piece of white cloth, and plunged the blade into the left side of his abdomen. Blood gushed from the wound, but without uttering a sound he sliced across to the right side, pulled out the blade for an instant, and plunged it in again, repeating the process in the opposite direction. With the third slice, he released a guttural wail, his only means to summon a final burst of strength. But his *seppuku* was not complete until he deliberately placed the bloody dagger at his right side, and fell forward with both hands extended directly in front of him. The next instant the seconds drew their long swords, piercing the heart of their beloved sword master. Takechi Zuizan was dead at age thirty-six; and so nobly did he perform his *seppuku*, displaying his inner purity, that his enemies were left speechless.

A
Soul-Encompassing
Dread

Settings

An open field somewhere in the province of Mito, autumn 1862

Several places in the Imperial capital and nearby Osaka, summer and fall of 1863

Players

Serizawa Kamo (*S*): A Mito samurai, expert swordsman, and commander of the Shinsengumi (a shogunal police corps)

Kondo Isami (*S*): An expert swordsman, and commander of the Shinsengumi

Hijikata Toshizo (*S*): An expert swordsman, and Kondo's closest friend and confidant

O-ume: Serizawa's mistress

A Soul-Encompassing Dread

It is a soul-encompassing dread which possesses a man faced with encroaching and certain death. When the cause of his imminent demise is an incurable disease, a man's reaction is, upon occasion, an uncontrollable anger directed at souls more fortunate than his. If the man is endowed with a particularly strong ego whereby he believes himself superior to or of a higher order than his fellow human beings, this anger most often transforms into a vicious rage which is apt to manifest itself as crazed violence, and in extreme instances, cold-blooded murder.

"Place these three men in a line twenty paces apart from one another," the tall, large man hollered angrily at a subordinate one cold afternoon. The tall, large man's name was Serizawa Kamo, formerly a samurai of the Mito clan, more recently a *ronin* of the same. Before becoming a commander of a dread shogunal police corps in the following March, Serizawa was now, in the late autumn of 1862, serving as captain of a rebel group with some three hundred Mito men under him. He was light of complexion, with small, dark eyes which penetrated the defenses of his many adversaries. He was gallant, yet brutal. Courageous, yet cruel. Charismatic, yet reckless. A madman, and the pampered youngest child of a well-to-do family. An expert swordsman of the Shinto Munen Style who regularly resorted to brute strength. A man of good breeding, and a pathological drinker who was wont to scream at the top of his lungs at the slightest provocation. Short-tempered, selfish, aggressive. A bold, dominant man of consequence who had his way with women, including other men's wives. Evil incarnate. Thus was the reputation of the enigmatic Serizawa Kamo. While he had laid bare his wretched soul over the thirty-some years of his short, volatile life, he harbored a gnawing, deep, dark secret within, which he would take with him to his grave. Serizawa was slowly dying from syphilis.

Serizawa had been drinking since morning on this cold day in late autumn, as was his custom. When he drank he became violent, lost control of himself, and, upon occasion, was known to draw his deadly sword. Earlier in the day he had had a difference of opinion with three of his men. The three unfortunates now stood in an open field of thick grass, some twenty paces apart from one another, their swords sheathed at their sides, and, as if resolved to their miserable fate, grimly calm. Serizawa positioned himself about ten paces from the first man, smiled wickedly, and slowly drew his long sword. Releasing an ear-piercing guttural wail, he charged the staggered line. The next instant three heads lay in the thick grass, blood spurting from the torsos.

Several years before, Serizawa had raped the wife of a wealthy merchant in his native Mito. His virulence and brute strength apparently had a bewitching effect, because, once violated, the woman became enraptured and begged Serizawa to keep her with him. He took advantage of the woman's weakness, and continued to ravage her for the next half year. Then one day he found that his appetite for her had been fully satiated. He told her to leave. When the woman readily obeyed, saying that she would return to the home of the wealthy merchant, Serizawa flew into a jealous rage. He took her to a nearby riverbank, made short work of her with his sword, and threw the bloody corpse into the raging stream.

Serizawa's brutality new no bounds. It was rumored that he had punished several wrongdoers among the Mito rebels by cutting off their fingers, hands, noses or ears, before banishing them from their camp. The Mito clan was one of the elite Three Tokugawa Branch Houses. The Lord of Mito had a reputation to keep, and could not indulge such behavior from one of his own. His brother, Lord Yoshinobu, would soon be appointed the Bakufu's Inspector General of the Forces to Protect the Emperor, and some three years hence become the fifteenth and last Tokugawa Shogun. When word of Serizawa's most recent atrocities reached the authorities in Edo, he was arrested, brought to the Shogun's capital, and sentenced to death. In the frigid coldness of his dark, dank jail cell he refused to eat. A patch of leaden late winter sky was barely visible through a small window, and his mind drifted to the snowy landscape beyond the grim prison walls. He called for a brush and ink. When his request was refused, he bit open his small finger and, with his blood, composed a farewell song, in defiance of his captors, this wretched world and his own imminent death.

Amidst the desolation of snow and frost,
   the plum is the first to bloom in brilliant color.
The blossoms keep their fragrance,
   even after they have scattered.

As fate had it, Serizawa Kamo's life would not yet be scattered in the relentless winds of eternity. Just before he was to be brought to the scaffold, it was decided by the Edo government that an entirely new type of police corps would be formed to patrol the Imperial capital. This corps would be called the Shinsengumi. Unlike existing police corps, whose ranks consisted of the sons of direct Bakufu retainers, the Shinsengumi would be made up entirely of *ronin*, the toughest who could be enlisted. They would restore peace to the blood-soaked streets of Kyoto, by killing or arresting other *ronin*. To this purpose the Shogunate proclaimed a general amnesty, whereby *ronin* who had been incarcerated were set free to enlist in the new corps. Needless to say, Serizawa jumped at the chance, and brought with him several of his cohorts from the Mito rebellion.

      *   *   *

In August 1863, five months after Serizawa was appointed as one of the three commanders of the Shinsengumi, an event took place in Kyoto that intensified the turmoil which had embroiled the Japanese nation for the past decade. The event was a *coup d'etat* at the very gates of the Imperial Palace, which resulted in a dramatic reversal in the power play between the Choshu-led Loyalists who advocated *Toppling the Bakufu and Imperial Loyalism*, and the Bakufu supporters who espoused a *Union of Court and Camp*. On the night of August eighteenth, heavily armed Satsuma and Aizu troops seized the Nine Forbidden Gates of the Imperial Palace, which had thus far been guarded by Choshu. Troops from five other clans joined Aizu and Satsuma, barring entrance to the palace by radical court nobles, Choshu samurai and all other Loyalists. In the still of the night the boom of a single cannon shot informed the Emperor that the palace had been completely sealed off, and awoke the startled champions of *Imperial Loyalism* at court, who now discovered that they no longer had access to the Son of Heaven. As the Choshu troops aimed their cannon at the palace, they received an Imperial order to retreat or else be branded an "Imperial Enemy." The political stage in Kyoto had taken a complete turnabout in a single night, as the men of the Tokugawa once again ruled the Imperial capital.

The Shinsengumi was placed under the control of the powerful Lord of Aizu, who was the Bakufu's Protector of Kyoto, a cousin of the Shogun and staunch supporter of the Tokugawa. As the coup in Kyoto was unfolding, the newly formed corps received orders to report to Hamaguri Gate, one of the Nine Forbidden Gates. Here the Shinsengumi would get its first taste of war, assisting the Aizu and Satsuma troops against the forces of Choshu. Eighty men of the Shinsengumi formed two columns. At their front flew the corps' white banner, some four feet long and three feet wide, emblazoned in red with the Chinese character for "sincerity." The rank and file wore jackets of pale yellow with broad stripes on the sleeves and pleated gray trousers, while the three commanders were clad in ominous black. Each man wore a white war headband tied at the back, and all bore swords at their left hip. Some wielded lethal spears, while Commander Serizawa carried a heavy iron-ribbed fan in his sash etched with the slogan "loyalty and patriotism."

"Identify yourselves," demanded one of a group of Aizu samurai guarding Hamaguri Gate. The Aizu men held spears, which they now pointed at the oncoming procession.

The two columns halted suddenly. They were confused. They had expected to be welcomed as comrades-in-arms, but instead were treated as enemies. While the two other corps commanders were outwardly startled, Serizawa maintained his composure, and answered defiantly, "We are the Shinsengumi, under the authority of the Lord of Aizu. We have just received orders to report to the palace, and are going in now." With one of the Aizu spears held six inches from his face, Serizawa laughed derisively, drew the iron-ribbed fan from his sash, and with one sharp motion brushed the blade aside.

"The Shinsengumi," the startled Aizu man said. "Please excuse our impertinence."

In the previous month, Serizawa and some others had been sent to the nearby mercantile capital of Osaka, to arrest or kill anti-Bakufu Loyalists recently gathering there. With the rebel and government forces about to clash in a *coup d'etat* in Kyoto, the entire Osaka-Kyoto area was one of mounting tension.

The evening of July fifteenth was scorching. To escape the heat, Serizawa and seven others had hired a pleasure boat on the Yodogawa river. There was a full moon, and the men drank *sake* aboard the boat. Upon landing, they headed for the nearby pleasure quarter to enjoy the rest of the night. They were dressed casually, some in short hemp trousers and frocks, others in dark blue cotton robes and pleated trousers worn for fencing practice. As the eight swordsmen walked down a narrow alleyway toward a favorite brothel, they confronted a lone sumo wrestler steadily approaching from the opposite direction. The wrestler, who was much larger than any of them, was undaunted. To him the crudely dressed group appeared as mere ruffians who did not warrant his attention. He had no idea that they were impeccable swordsman who would not hesitate to utilize their license to kill.

"Move aside," Serizawa ordered.

"What did you say?" the wrestler responded belligerently. Serizawa drew his short sword, and, in the same motion, sliced open the wrestler's chest, killing him instantly. Without looking back, the group continued on their way to the brothel.

As the eight men sat on the tatami in a private room, drinking *sake* with as many kimono-clad harlots, a group of twenty-one sumo wrestlers armed with heavy wooden clubs barged in upon them. "We avenge the murder of our brother," they hollered. The swordsmen immediately drew their blades, which glistened in the light from the full moon shining through an open window. The women stood up screaming, and when they tried to flee were knocked down amidst the ensuing pandemonium. Blood spurted from one wrestler's neck, another's hand was hacked off at the wrist, and three more screamed in agony. Calm was only restored after five wrestlers lay dead, and the sixteen others, some severely wounded, fled for their lives. One of the Shinsengumi received a club wound to the chest, another on the side of the head, and a third swordsman was accidentally cut on the left arm by the tip of a comrade's blade.

The magistrates in charge of keeping the peace in Osaka and Kyoto were vexed at the behavior of the Shinsengumi, but powerless in the face of the increasing authority wielded by Serizawa and his unruly band. As the power of the Shinsengumi grew, so did the special privileges enjoyed by its commanders. Serizawa now found himself virtually above the rule of law, free to wreak terror on anyone who aroused his ire. During the summer of 1863, an official of the Minakuchi clan, whose *daimyo* was a direct retainer of the Shogun, paid a visit to the Kyoto estate of the Lord of Aizu to complain about the violent behavior of the Shinsengumi. When word of this reached Serizawa, he flew into a rage. "Let's go get the son of a bitch," he told several of his men, with whom he immediately set out to the Minakuchi estate. Waiting for their arrival was a well-known sword master. The sword master had been advised of Serizawa's murderous intent, and, being a peaceful man, took it upon himself to convince his colleague in the way of the sword to drop the matter.

"Let's go to the Sumiya and cool off," the sword master suggested. The Sumiya was a house located in Shimabara, a licensed pleasure quarter of Kyoto. Soon the party arrived at the brothel, where they were provided with a large private room encompassing twenty-eight tatami mats. The room was equipped with numerous low wooden tables set with fine porcelain and lacquer ware, on which were served the condiments of superb Kyoto *sake*. In a wooden alcove built into one of the walls was a splendid ceramic vase, adorned with two purple and delicate Japanese bellflowers. On the wall behind the vase hung an exquisite scroll of a Chinese landscape in black ink. With the men were a dozen young women in bright kimono, whose duties, among others less defined, included keeping *sake* cups full. After a short time Serizawa became drunk. When drunk, he was easily offended, at which time he would become enraged and absolutely out of control, a result of the syphilis which had spread to his brain. "More *sake*," he screamed, taking his empty cup and hurling it into the alcove. As the others looked on in dismay, unable to control their commander, Serizawa drew his iron-ribbed fan from his sash, and with one violent motion, cleared one of the tables of porcelain and lacquer ware. When the frightened women attempted to leave the room, Serizawa stood up, knocked several of them down, as the others wept hysterically. After similarly clearing the rest of the tables, the madman now went to the alcove, where he destroyed the hanging scroll, and with his iron-ribbed fan smashed the fine ceramic vase. When there was nothing left for him to destroy in this room, he stormed through the paper screen door, tearing the wooden frame from the threshold, then raced up a stairway. He ripped out part of the railing along the corridor of the second floor, and ran with it downstairs, where he used it as a club to smash large casks of *sake*. Next he went into the kitchen and smashed every dish in sight. Although the occupants and workers of the house had fled the scene unharmed, the Sumiya was left in shambles. Serizawa's rage was not abated until he had the proprietor of the Sumiya placed under house confinement for one week, for "inexcusable behavior."

*   *   *

That Serizawa Kamo was endowed with a particularly large ego cannot be disputed. Nor is there any room for doubt that he believed himself superior to and even of a higher order than his fellow human beings. That he had repeatedly violated the code of the samurai was a blatant fact. That he was a cruel, uncivilized brute with a propensity for cold-blooded murder is unquestionable. But whether or not he was evil warrants argument. No less an authority on the human psyche than Sigmund Freud maintains that the behavior of even the most heinous murderer is merely an expression of his individual liberty. "The liberty of the individual is not a benefit of culture," says Freud.* Nor is a license for murder, rape, extortion, or any other of the crimes which Serizawa openly committed. Perhaps these crimes represent the discontents inherent in civilization, a fundamental condition for which, Freud says, is the "substitution of power of a united number [of people] for the power of a single man." Freud has more to say on the subject: "The desire for freedom may...have its origin in the primitive roots of the personality, still unfettered by civilizing influences, and so become a source of antagonism to culture." Does the possibility not exist that a

---

**Civilization and Its Discontents*, 1929 (translated by Joan Riviere) *certain type of man, the uncivilized brute who commits the most barbarous of crimes, is not inherently evil, but is merely acting out of his natural instinct to fend for or improve himself, and therefore unable not to commit atrocities? Or perhaps he is merely reacting to a deep, dark dread which encompasses his soul.*

*   *   *

That deep, dark dread seemed to be at work once again on August thirteenth. Serizawa and several others paid a visit to the offices of a wealthy Kyoto establishment called the Yamato-ya. Commander Serizawa had heard that anti-Bakufu Loyalist forces had recently extorted money from the Yamato-ya on the grounds that the merchant house had been dealing with "filthy barbarians". "If the Yamato-ya is willing to finance renegades who are trying to overthrow the Bakufu, they had better give us some money too," Serizawa told his men.

The proprietor of the Yamato-ya simply refused the Shinsengumi demands. Threatening the merchant house that "law and order are not free of charge," Serizawa took drastic measures. He led his men back to Shinsengumi headquarters, and returned in the evening with a cannon in tow. They fired several rounds on the Yamato-ya's large storehouse, intending to burn it to the ground. The wooden and earthen structure, however, did not burn as easily as they had assumed. When some of the nearby buildings caught fire instead, the bell sounded in the fire tower. When the fire brigade arrived at the scene, the men of the Shinsengumi trained their rifles on them. "If you so much as throw one bucketful of water on the blaze," they hollered, "we'll shoot." Watching the scene from the rooftop of a nearby building was Commander Serizawa, laughing hysterically. Serizawa and his men continued the uproar throughout the night and well into the next day, until they had entirely destroyed the storehouse.

"Damn it," seethed the Lord of Aizu upon hearing of Serizawa's latest offense. The Protector of Kyoto was, needless to say, very unhappy that his police corps behaved contrary to its *raison d'être*. He summoned five men of the Shinsengumi to his official residence. Among them were Kondo Isami, who was one of the three corps commanders, and Hijikata Toshizo, Kondo's closest friend and confidant. All five were expert swordsmen formerly of Kondo's fencing academy in the province of Musashi. None of these men, who made up the crux of Commander Kondo's faction within the Shinsengumi, approved of Commander Serizawa's behavior. Unlike Serizawa, Kondo and Hijikata hailed from peasant households. They had been elevated to samurai status in recognition of their superior martial skills. That they now found themselves at the helm of a Tokugawa police corps was nothing short of miraculous, and they were poignantly aware that their rise to power was only made possible by the bloody times it had been theirs to inherit. They rightly felt that Serizawa's behavior jeopardized the very existence of their corps, which had become their very reason for living. "Without the corps," they told each other, "we'd have nothing." Over these past several months, they had silently been waiting for an opportunity to eliminate the Serizawa faction. When the Lord of Aizu ordered them to do just that, they wasted no time in laying their assassination plans.

Serizawa was notorious for his violation of women. It is said that as a boy he had raped three maidservants at his family's home, so that each of them were pregnant at the same time. As commander of the Shinsengumi, he became enamored of the lover of one of his own men. The woman was a famous beauty, and Serizawa told the man that he would have his way with her. Shortly after, when the man was murdered by one of Serizawa's cohorts, the woman committed suicide.

The final victim of Serizawa's sexual transgressions was the wife of the owner of a fashionable kimono shop in Kyoto. A stylish dresser, Serizawa had charged a sizable sum of money for merchandise at this shop. But since he believed that his was a superior existence to that of a lowly merchant, and that as commander of the Shinsengumi he was above the rule of law, he simply refused to pay. "I risk my life daily to restore order to the streets of Kyoto," he rationalized.

The shop owner was at his wit's end trying to collect his money, until he heard that Serizawa was a man who loved women. In hopes that he had discovered a means by which he could convince the notorious swordsman to pay his debt, he sent his voluptuous wife, O-ume, to collect the bill. Certainly he knew nothing of the nature of the brute, for he very naively reasoned that Serizawa could be charmed into simply paying. When O-ume visited Serizawa's private room at Shinsengumi headquarters, he was delighted to see her. She was dressed in a beautiful kimono of bright colored silk, and her perfumed powder only whetted his appetite. He invited the woman inside, and, with *sake* cup in hand, entertained her entreaties that he pay his debt. After O-ume had finished speaking, and without further ado, Serizawa grabbed her with one arm and brought her down to the tatami. He easily overpowered her with the weight of his body, and with one hand untied the knot of her silk sash. When she protested he slapped her hard in the face, then unwound the sash from her midriff. As he removed her kimono she began to scream, but was immediately silenced and finally subdued by another slap in the face. Just as was the case with the wife of the wealthy merchant in Mito whose life he had plunged into tragedy, Serizawa's virulence and brute strength enraptured O-ume. After the rape, she visited him often. She begged him to take her as his mistress. When Serizawa acquiesced, O-ume left her husband.

The attack came in the still of the night of September eighteenth, as a hard rain pelted the tile roof above Serizawa's private room at Shinsengumi headquarters. He slept soundly with

O-ume in his arms, inebriated from too much drink and carnally satiated from the voluptuous body of his new lover. His bed was enclosed by a six-fold screen, and laid out atop the tatami. In an adjacent room were two of Serizawa's allies in the corps, both accompanied by harlots. One of the harlots got up to go to the latrine. As she opened the sliding screen door of the bedroom, she was confronted in the darkness by four men wielding drawn swords. "Save yourself and get out of here," one of them whispered.

The attack on Serizawa had been meticulously planned, so that he would not have a chance to defend himself. As he struggled to get up, his assailants covered him with the six-fold screen, through which they stabbed him repeatedly with their swords. They silenced the screaming woman with one clean stroke. Her head was severed from her body save a thin strip of skin at the back of her neck, and her blood covered the ceiling above. In the adjacent room one of Serizawa's two allies had been stabbed twice, although neither of his wounds were fatal. He and the harlot at his side only survived the attack by feigning death. The other man, whose companion had fled the scene, was killed instantly.

With the Serizawa faction eliminated, Kondo and Hijikata gained undisputed control of the Shinsengumi. Under their austere command the corps would soon become the most feared police force in Tokugawa history.

The Code

Settings

A cottage in the outskirts of Kyoto, one cold winter evening in 1866

The Ikedaya (an inn in Kyoto)

Headquarters of the Shinsengumi (a shogunal police corps)

Players

Tauchi Tomo (*S*): A rank-and-file member of the Shinsengumi

Kondo Isami (*S*): Commander of the Shinsengumi, and an expert swordsman

Hijikata Toshizo (*S*): Vice-commander of the Shinsengumi, and an expert swordsman

The Code

The most feared police force in Tokugawa history consisted of hundreds of expert swordsmen, each endowed with the official sanction and an unflinching propensity to kill. Their purpose: to restore law and order to the blood-soaked streets of the Imperial capital. "Fight fire with fire, and terror with terror," reasoned the powers that were, with a single-minded objective bolstered by the corps' draconian code.

The samurai, exhausted after long hours of duty, returned to the small cottage of his young mistress in the outskirts of Kyoto. He was particularly tired on this cold winter evening in 1866, for he had single-handedly cut down three among the hordes of renegades who had turned the formerly tranquil city into a blood-bath of political upheaval and terror.

The samurai wore the uniform of the Shinsengumi — a pale yellow jacket with broad strips on the sleeves, and pleated gray trousers. The Shinsengumi had been formed to destroy the enemies of the Tokugawa Shogun. The Shogun's enemies were self-styled *Men of High Purpose* intent on overthrowing his military regime. The majority of their ranks hailed from the powerful Satsuma, Choshu and Tosa clans, which stood at the vanguard of the revolution. Many of them were *ronin* — renegade samurai who had unlawfully fled their clans to join the revolutionary forces in the Imperial capital — and all were dedicated to the holy cause of restoring the Son of Heaven to power.

The samurai's name was Tauchi Tomo. He had been recruited by the Shinsengumi for his expertise with a sword, his penchant for cold-blooded murder, and his oath to die rather than let an enemy escape.

Tauchi's mistress was a harlot whom he had found at a brothel in the Shimabara pleasure quarter, and engaged to serve his needs and no one else's. She wore a plain kimono of dark blue cotton, a yellow sash around her midriff, and her long black hair tied up neatly at the crown of her small head.

The tiny cottage in which the samurai kept his mistress was surrounded by open fields, and in the winter exposed to the biting, cold winds which blew in from the north. The cottage consisted of two simple matted rooms, a kitchen, and a bath. The young woman nervously greeted her master at the entrance of the cottage, offered him a bucket of clean hot water to wash his feet, and in a slightly strained tone bid him remove his two swords. "Here, let me take them from you," she said. "You look so tired."

"Stupid woman," the samurai said derisively. "I've told you many times that corps regulations forbid me to hand my swords over to anyone."

The conduct of the men of the Shinsengumi was ruled by the iron will of their two leaders, Kondo Isami and Hijikata Toshizo. Both were expert swordsmen from the province of Musashi, just southwest of the Shogun's capital of Edo. Their resolve to die in the service of the Bakufu was unsurpassed. Commander Kondo had been master of the Kondo Fencing Academy in his home province, Vice-commander Hijikata his right-hand man. Neither of these leaders of two-sworded men had been born into the samurai class. Both hailed from peasant households, and notwithstanding their humble origins, had recently been granted the high privilege of direct access to the Shogun.

The Shinsengumi had been established in the spring of 1863 under the control of the powerful Lord of Aizu, whose Matsudaira family crest displayed the three hollyhock leaves of the Tokugawa. Unlike other Bakufu police corps, which consisted mainly of samurai from the elite classes of Tokugawa retainers, the Shinsengumi was made up entirely of *ronin*. For their loyal service, each of the some two hundred fifty men of the Shinsengumi received a generous monthly stipend, and in the summer of 1867 would become direct retainers of the Shogun. As suggested by the corps' symbol — the Chinese character for "sincerity" — its leaders commanded their corps based on the severest of codes. Strictly prohibited were "violating the code of the samurai," "quitting the corps," "raising money for selfish purposes," and "fighting for personal reasons." Violation of any of these prohibitions was punishable by death — beheading or, if the condemned man warranted more honorable treatment, self-disembowelment. Attached to the prohibitions was a list of regulations, one of which stated: "If any member of the corps should draw his sword, he must kill his opponent. If he merely wounds him and let's him escape, he must commit *seppuku*."

To accommodate an increase in its ranks, during the previous spring the Shinsengumi had moved headquarters from the Mibu district in the western outskirts of Kyoto to a more accessible location in a spacious meeting hall in the precincts of a nearby Buddhist temple. The meeting hall had thus far been used for housing monks gathered from throughout Japan to this center of Buddhist learning. The Shinsengumi partitioned off the hall to form barracks for its men. Between the main temple hall and headquarters, the corps constructed a bathhouse, a jail and execution grounds for beheading captured renegades and certain of its own men who had failed to abide by the code.

Recently, Kondo and Hijikata had decided that a partitioned temple hall was inadequate as living quarters for their men, and that accommodations more suitable for preserving the dignity of the corps were needed. They planned to construct new headquarters which would rival in grandeur the Kyoto estates of even the most powerful feudal lords. As funding was the greatest obstacle to their plan, they devised a scheme to convince the good priests of the temple to offer financial assistance. In plain view of the main hall, men of the Shinsengumi who had violated the code were ordered to commit *seppuku*, captured enemies were tortured and executed amidst shrieks of pain, and innocent townspeople were brutalized. "Priests simply don't have the stomach for violence," they assured each other. "It's only a matter of time before they give in." Their reasoning was correct, and not entirely evil. After all, the men of the Shinsengumi were risking their lives daily to restore law and order to the Imperial capital, and to preserve the government of the Tokugawa Shogun, whose family had ruled Japan peacefully for centuries, and on whose well-being their livelihood and even lives now depended.

Tauchi sat down on a raised wooden platform at the entrance to the cottage. His jacket was streaked here and there with blood and mud, frozen from the cold outside.

"You're filthy," the woman said, grimacing. Her tone of voice unsettled the samurai, although he knew not why.

"Strange," he thought, as he removed his straw sandals, placed one foot at a time into the bucket of hot water, and recalled the blood which earlier in the day had splashed on the white earthen exterior wall of a latticed house on a narrow back street near the Kamogawa river. "Killing men has become easier than enduring this woman."

Since enlisting in the Shinsengumi, killing men had not only become easy for Tauchi, but indeed a passion and his greatest purpose. His first taste of bloodshed came with the Slaughter at the Ikedaya, where in June 1864, the Shinsengumi had attacked a gathering of rebels, and thereby secured its notoriety. The rebels, under the leadership of the Choshu clan, were planning to overthrow the government. The plan was squelched when, on the previous night, Commander Kondo and several others had raided the Kyoto home of a rebel leader, confiscating a cache of guns and ammunition.

The night of June fifth was sweltering. The town was alive with celebration on this eve of the annual Gion Festival. The streets were lit with hundreds of paper lanterns, glowing red and white in front of latticed shops, teahouses, restaurants and inns. The steady pounding of drums, the winding of flutes, the continuous clanging of brass bells filled the humid air. One of these inns, the Ikedaya, was the secret meeting place for twenty

Imperial Loyalists. The rebels were huddled together, drinking *sake* in a second-story room as they finalized their war plans. The innkeeper was a Loyalist sympathizer, so that the rebels had little reason to suspect that the manservant who served them *sake* and who now offered to put their long swords in an adjacent room to make more space for their ranks, was actually a spy of the Shinsengumi.

The slaughter came shortly after the rebels had relinquished their swords. Eight expert swordsmen, as resolved to die to protect the Shogunate as the rebels were to destroy it, stole silently through the front gate of the Ikedaya. They stormed through the front door, and by the time the rebels upstairs, armed only with their short swords, realized they were under attack, the men of the Shinsengumi were upon them.

Tauchi stood up, scowled slightly. "Prepare a bath," he told the woman, unlatching the sheath of his sword. The woman flinched as the samurai drew the blade from the scabbard, then raised it up to take a closer look. "That's fine," he said to himself, recalling the badly nicked edge of the sword he had replaced after the Slaughter at the Ikedaya. "The Ikedaya," he sighed nostalgically.

Resheathing the blade with a loud clang, the samurai removed both swords from his left hip, then entered the adjacent room. He sat down at a low wooden table on badly worn tatami, placed his swords at his left side, and leaned back against the sliding doors of a closet. He stared at the alcove in the opposite wall, decorated plainly with an empty ceramic flower vase. The room was dimly lit with a single paper lantern. The earthen walls were bare; the only furniture the lantern, a pale gray ceramic brazier, and the low wooden table, onto which he now leaned over to rest his head.

"I'll bring some *sake* first," the woman said nervously, before quickly leaving the room.

"Yes, *sake*," the samurai said, closed his eyes and vividly recalled the rush of power he felt the first time he had killed a man. The bloodcurdling wail. The ecstasy of overpowering his victim. The sensation of pulling razor-sharp steel through muscle. The screeching sound of the blade cutting through bone. The gurgle of blood spurting from the body. The debris of human flesh scattered about. The headless corpse, and the severed head which he had nearly tripped over in pursuit of the enemy. The coppery, sweet smell of blood and sweat amidst the uproar of heated battle which left dead eleven of the rebels, three of the Shinsengumi and fifteen from the ranks of other shogunal troops. And never a pang of guilt for the numerous men he had killed since the Ikedaya slaughter. After all, he was a member of the Shinsengumi, whose purpose for existence was to maintain order in the sacred Imperial capital.

Tauchi felt something wet on the tabletop, and raised his head. "Melted blood," he said, wiping the side of his face with his hand. Then noticing a distinct sweet fragrance which was not that of blood, said, "And *sake*. Who's been...." Before he could finish speaking his thoughts, the closet doors burst open, and his brain screamed from a sharp icy pain on his left shoulder. Tauchi grabbed his long sword, stood up to face his assailant, only to be brought down by a second attack to the legs. He lay face up in a pool of blood, and noticed the red splash that covered the wooden ceiling. When he heard the strained voices of a man and woman fleeing through the front door, he tried to get up but could not, as the sweet fragrance of blood mixed with *sake* now sickened him.

Tauchi regained consciousness some time later. He was very cold and quite alone. He attempted to move his arms to warm himself, but the biting pain in his shoulder and legs prohibited him. He screamed to attract attention. When help finally arrived he sent word to Shinsengumi headquarters of what had happened, but not without a fast feeling of dread. Soon a palanquin arrived to bring him back to headquarters, where Commander Kondo and Vice-commander Hijikata were waiting.

"Imbecile," Kondo screamed at the sight of the bloodied man, held upright by two others on either side. "You have allowed an enemy to cut you and escape unscathed?"

"Yes," Tauchi answered, wincing as much from shame as the pain of his gaping wounds.

"Then you have violated the code."

"Yes," Tauchi acknowledged grimly, dropping his head.

"Based on corps regulations, I hereby order you to commit *seppuku*. Choose your second. The sentence is to be carried out immediately."

The Execution
Grounds

Settings
The scaffold at the official execution grounds in Edo,
December 1860

A tea shop in a busy section of modern downtown Tokyo

Player
Yamada Asaemon VII (aka "The Beheader"): The Shogunate's
unofficial executioner, and the Shogun's designated sword-
tester

The Execution Grounds

During the years of chaos before the fall of the Tokugawa, the formerly peaceful streets of the Shogun's capital became scenes of unprecedented bloodshed. Political assassins terrorized the city, cutting down supporters of the Bakufu and their suspected sympathizers with equal vengeance. Enemies of the Tokugawa were arrested and thrown in jail among common criminals, and official beheadings became a daily occurrence. Samurai who had never before drawn their blades in battle now wore their two swords with a newfound propensity to use them.

The indispensability of a sharp blade was by no means limited to times of battle. One official executioner, having beheaded six thousand men over a span of thirty years, could judge the efficiency of a sword by the sight of the blade, or the sound it made severing a head from the body. Indeed, the executioner's sword was every bit as lethal as the warrior's, as was his swordsmanship. And perhaps this grim truth was nowhere more clearly demonstrated than at the official execution grounds in Edo.

In the summer of 1853, Commodore Matthew Perry of the United States Navy led a squadron of four heavily armed warships into Sagami Bay, just south of Edo, demanding that Japan end two and a half centuries of isolation. Five years later, Ii Naosuke, the powerful regent to the Shogun, authorized Japan's first commercial treaty with a foreign nation, arousing sharp opposition among xenophobic samurai throughout Japan. The regent subsequently unleashed a reign of terror in the form of the wholesale arrest or execution of his political enemies. On an unseasonably snowy morning in the spring of 1860, Ii was assassinated at the gates of Edo Castle, and now, in late December of the same year, the Shogun's capital, and indeed the entire Japanese nation, reeled in turmoil.

While the death sentence was regularly handed down for the

more serious crimes of treason and murder, those convicted of petty theft exceeding a value of ten gold coins, or fraud for a lesser amount, were equally as certain to be brought to the scaffold. The priest of a particular Buddhist temple in Edo during this time is said to have performed funeral rites for sixty thousand executed men. Yamada Asaemon VII, the Shogunate's unofficial executioner, had personally beheaded thousands since inheriting his position twelve years before, in 1848. Recently, the "Beheader," as the patriarch of the Yamada family was known, had cut off the head of Yoshida Shoin, the martyred revolutionary teacher from the great domain of Choshu. Although there had been a sudden rise in the number of executions over these past two years, the final days of each year were exceptionally demanding for Yamada. The authorities in Edo were eager to empty the jails of condemned criminals before the New Year, and Yamada was the only man commissioned by the government to behead them.

Now, on this cold, clear morning in late December, Yamada, whose given name was Yoshitoshi, stood in an open courtyard adjacent to the prison, deliberately studying the mien of the terrified man brought to the scaffold some ten paces before him. The prisoner appeared young, perhaps in his late twenties, although Yamada could not be sure for the soft strip of white paper cloth which covered the condemned man's eyes. A coarse rope had been placed around the prisoner's neck, and his arms were tightly bound at both sides with heavy rope wound around his torso. "One more," Yamada thought, calmly placing his right hand on the hilt of his sword. This was the seventh man brought to the scaffold this morning. The other six had been murderers or thieves, but earlier this morning Yamada had been informed that this last man must die for the crime of "sexual infatuation for another man's wife." The young man had seduced the woman, whose husband was the owner of a dry goods shop in Edo's Asakusa district. Their illicit affair had been uncovered by another, much younger woman who worked for the husband,

and who had also been seduced by the same young man. One day while the husband was away on business, the younger woman walked into the private quarters above the dry goods shop. When she discovered her master's wife in a sexual act with her unfaithful lover, she flew into a jealous rage, and, such is the fury of the female beast, immediately reported her discovery to the office of the local magistrate. When the crime became public, the cuckold man was so shamed that he closed his shop, packed what belongings he could carry, and left with this wife to resume life in her native countryside.

The Beheader was the master of the Yamada Style of fencing, which required not only pinpoint precision for instantaneous death as the least painful method of severing the head from the body, but also that four prescribed Buddhist precepts be silently recited as the Beheader drew his blade. The purpose for reciting these precepts was dual: to cleanse the mind of worldly thoughts, and to maintain composure, concentrating one's mental energy at the pit of the abdomen, below the navel. Although Yamada Asaemon VII did not share the vulgar belief in vengeful hauntings by spirits of the dead, he had another, more personal motive for appeasing the souls of the people whom he beheaded. For seven generations the patriarch of the Yamada family had enjoyed the exclusive right to take the liver from the dead body of each criminal he had executed. Human liver was a valuable commodity which could only be taken from the corpse of an executed man. It was used as an ingredient in a medicine which was commonly believed could cure a wide range of ailments. This medicine was manufactured and sold exclusively by the Yamada family, who were grateful for this important source of livelihood.

Yamada's unsavory trade notwithstanding, he was a proud man. His pride rested in the repute afforded by his principal profession of designated sword-tester to the Tokugawa Shogun. The role of beheader was merely a side occupation his ancestor had accepted upon his appointment as shogunal sword-tester in

1737. Since the practical purpose of a sword was to cut one's enemies, its effectiveness could only be confirmed on a human body, and not on bundles of straw, wooden poles or the bodies of animals. In some cases the live body of a condemned criminal was used, in others an executed corpse. Accordingly, the roles of sword-tester and beheader were naturally performed by the same person. The official executioner was a Tokugawa retainer whose family patriarch had held that post for generations, but whose skill with a sword and propensity to use one lagged far behind seven consecutive generations of men by the name of Yamada Asaemon. The Yamada were a family of *ronin*, lordless samurai, who for over a century had plied their trade at the official execution grounds in the Kodenma-cho district of Edo.

The condemned man, shivering in spasmodic jerks, was now asked, as a matter of course, his name, age and place of birth. His identity reconfirmed, he was forced to kneel atop a straw mat which had been placed before the scaffold. Standing nearby was the Beheader, dressed in a gray kimono under a formal black jacket displaying the Yamada family crest of the holly. Stuck through his sash, at his left hip, were his long and short swords. With the prisoner were five outcasts, men whose family had been forbidden by their lowly birth any kind of social classification whatsoever. One of the outcasts produced a small knife with which he cut the ropes from the condemned man's neck and torso. Three of them now positioned themselves behind the prisoner, while the other two, remaining at either side of the condemned, loosened his short cotton frock. After baring the prisoner's shoulders, they turned up the bottom of his kimono to the base of the knees. This procedure they performed with the utmost of care. They would receive the dead man's clothes after the beheading, and they did not want them soiled with his blood.

Directly in front of the condemned man was a rectangular hole, measuring about three feet by six, and known in the vernacular as the "blood vat." This hole had been dug some three feet into the rich, dark earth, and sealed with white plaster. Covering the plaster was a piece a straw matting. The blood vat was surrounded by a frame of hard wood. There was a crescent-shaped indentation on one side of the frame, carved out by the point of the executioner's sword — testimony of the vast amount of blood which had recently flowed at the official execution grounds in Kodenma-cho. Placed nearby was a pail of water, over the handle of which had been hung pieces of soft white paper cloth.

The two outcasts positioned at either side of the prisoner now took firm hold of his arms. The three men behind the prisoner held his legs and pushed down on his back so that his head hung over the blood vat. Nearby, overseeing the entire process, stood the Inspector of the Execution. He was accompanied by the Commissioner of the Prison and the Chief Jailer. "Do you have any last wishes?" the Inspector of the Execution asked the criminal, an official gesture to which the condemned man was expected to answer negatively.

"Yes," the condemned man said, although he shivered violently. "I would like to be allowed to sleep with that woman just one more time."

The Inspector of the Execution frowned, casting a steely glance at the Beheader, who now calmly took his place at the scaffold. "All things impermanent," he uttered, as he wrapped his index finger around the hilt of his sword. "All things everchanging, never-ending," he whispered, firming his grip with his middle finger. "Freedom from life and death, attainment of extinction," he recited, placing his fourth finger around the hilt. "The bliss of nirvana," he concluded, and with this his grip was complete. The outcasts at the rear jerked hard the feet of the condemned man, who, shivering uncontrollably from the cold of the late winter morning and the terror which now consumed him, reacted by thrusting his head forward over the blood vat. The prisoner heaved violently as a sickly green stream gushed from his open mouth, and the late morning sunlight glistened off polished steel. The next instant came a sound like the snapping of a towel in the wind, and the severed head fell with a heavy thud onto the straw mat at the bottom of the blood vat. From the headless torso spewed a torrent of red, which the outcasts aimed directly into the hole, until, after four or five hard gushes, it gradually diminished to a trickle.

As four of the outcasts pressed the remaining blood from the corpse, the fifth one reached into the gore-filled hole, and took up the head by the topknot. He washed off the blood with a ladleful of clear water from the pail, then raised the head so that the left side faced the Inspector of the Execution, who nodded approval. Meanwhile Yamada rinsed the blood from his sword, and took a piece of soft white paper cloth from the handle of the pail. After wiping the blade he resheathed his sword, and instructed the outcasts to lay the corpse flat on its back. Drawing his short sword, Yamada made an incision above the navel, into which an outcast inserted his hand. Like an experienced butcher gutting the carcass of a dead animal, he removed the liver and immediately placed it into an earthen jar.

*   *   *

It is a cold, clear morning in late December. The elderly tea shop proprietress has just finished sweeping the sidewalk in front of her store, located in a busy section of the Kodenma-cho district in downtown Tokyo. The proprietress wears a clean white apron over her kimono, her gray hair neatly tied back. She is carefully dusting the packets of assorted teas, ceramic teacups and teapots that adorn the tidily arranged shelves of her quaint shop. The pleasant aroma of the roasted tea leaves which are her livelihood fills her with a warm sense of security and order in her life. Her happiness has recently been completed by the knowledge that her only grandson has been engaged to be married in the spring. The bride-to-be is the second daughter of a respectable family, whose patriarch made a fortune producing windshield wipers for automobiles during the years following World War II. Now the elderly proprietress can rest assured that her family line will continue, and that, although she rarely gives much thought to her own mortality, when the time comes there will be someone to attend her grave. The proprietress also takes comfort in the knowledge that at this time of year she will sell a large quantity of tea to the throngs which pass by her shop, all in a day in their busy lives.

Now the proprietress is talking amiably to a local matron who has come to purchase tea for her house guests during the New Year holiday. The two women are briefly interrupted by the friendly mailman, who has parked his red, post office-issue bicycle at the front of the shop. The mailman greets the two women with a warm smile, before handing a small bundle of mail to the proprietress, tipping his hat and busily taking his leave. Now a fashionably dressed young woman enters the shop. She is breathing heavily, as if out of breath. She has come to purchase some tea for her office, she says, all in a fluster. She would like to get something special, but is not sure which type to buy. The proprietress offers to prepare some samples, but the young woman declines, saying that she must hurry. It is the end of the year, she says, and everyone at her office is very busy. She purchases the same tea as usual, before hurrying on her way.

It is an historical fact that the Kodenma-cho district in the Shogun's capital of Edo served as the site of the official execution grounds for centuries. Government scribes recorded in painstaking detail thousands of names and functions of people who, in one way or another, assisted the executioner. Their ranks included jailers, constables, prison commissioners, fact verifiers, guards, overseers, execution inspectors, grounds keepers, and so on and so forth. There were, however, no historical records kept of the vast amount of blood which, despite the carefully contrived blood vats, had seeped into the rich, dark earth of Kodenma-cho, nor of the number of people who had been decapitated by the sharp swords of the patriarchs of eight generations of the Yamada family. But all of the government functionaries who so conscientiously fulfilled their important duties are now, of course, dead. Most of their records have been lost to the ravages of natural disaster or war. They might as well never have lived — the irony of which would have undoubtedly pleased the countless souls whom they collectively pushed over the brink to the other side of eternity.

But no matter. All is well in a mundane world. The rich, dark earth imbued with centuries of blood has long been covered over by the asphalt of modern Tokyo. It lies beneath the quaint shops run by tidy old women who sell their wares to local matrons and busy office girls, and is tread upon daily by the mass of humanity which are happily detached from the reality that one day they too must join the innumerable and long forgotten dead, so that their lives have always been and will continue to be quite and inexplicably meaningless.

Cutting Test

Settings
The cutting test area at the official execution grounds in Edo,
December 1860

Player
Yamada Asaemon VII (aka "The Beheader"): The Shogunate's
unofficial executioner, and the Shogun's designated sword-
tester

Cutting Test

During the bloody final years of the era of the samurai, a sharp blade was indispensable to the men who lived and died by the sword. The Japanese sword — a single-edged steel blade, curved and tempered to perfection — was a thing of beauty, and the most lethal cutting weapon produced by man. "The color of the stars on a frosty autumn night," sang a poet of old. "The color of the sky in March, when the cherries are in bloom. A Japanese sword drawn from its sheath. The beauty of a glowing tempered blade." The aesthetic allure of the Japanese sword was an incidental result of a meticulous tempering process by which the steel was repeatedly folded into tens of thousands of layers. The purpose of the Japanese sword, however, was simple: cutting the body of one's enemy.

A perfectly honed blade, of course, was only effective when wielded by a proficient swordsman. Contrarily, no matter how perfected a man's swordsmanship, without a perfectly honed blade he could not defend himself properly. It is said that Tokugawa Ieyasu, the first Shogun and founding father of the dynasty which bore his name, obtained immense enjoyment in watching cutting tests performed on live criminals. During the centuries of relative peace which followed Ieyasu's rule, the men of the warrior class gradually lost interest in the efficiency of their swords, and quite naturally the gruesome practice of cutting tests greatly diminished. There was a brief revival of cutting tests in the first half of the eighteenth century, under the eighth Shogun, Tokugawa Yoshimune. A great enthusiast of the martial arts, Yoshimune was known to summon to his palace the most skilled swordsmiths in all Japan. The blades they forged for the Shogun were tested on condemned criminals in the capital. It is said that Yoshimune personally inspected those blades which had passed the cutting tests, to check with his own eyes the condition of the edges which had severed human bone, and the steel which had been covered with warm human blood just hours or even moments before.

Notwithstanding Yoshimune's martial sentiments, the Tokugawa Period was, for the most part, one of sleepy peace, which ended with the sudden appearance of Commodore Perry's flotilla of "Black Ships" and the gunboat diplomacy which ensued. Fifteen years of bloody turmoil followed, during which samurai from clans throughout Japan clashed with men of the Tokugawa. Assassination became rampant in the Shogun's capital, and the practice of cutting tests was revived. A man who obtained a new sword needed to be sure that in case of a fight the blade would indeed be sharp enough to readily cut through the tough sinews and hard bone of his enemy. And as the Shogun's designated sword-tester, Yamada Asaemon VII now found his skills in unprecedented demand.

The condemned man's arms were tightly bound to his torso with heavy rope. Another rope was tied around his neck. He was blindfolded with a piece of soft white paper cloth, folded in two and tied behind his head with a small cord. He wore only a thin loin cloth of white cotton, despite the biting wind which blew in from the north on this cold, clear morning in late December. The prisoner had just been led by four outcasts into the official execution grounds in the Kodenma-cho district of Edo.

Yamada Asaemon VII stood near a sturdy wooden post, planted deeply into the rich, dark earth. Near the post were two bamboo poles tied together perpendicularly. One of the poles had been driven into the ground so that it was parallel to and some five feet away from the wooden post. The other pole was parallel to the ground, at a height just below Yamada's shoulders.

The sword-tester studied the prisoner carefully, as a bullfighter might a bull in his pen, or a butcher a pig as he prepared for the slaughter, to evaluate the degree of difficulty of the cutting test he was about to perform. He rarely performed a cutting test on a live person, but the owner of the sword which he now held in his right hand was a high-ranking Bakufu official whose special request he could not readily refuse. His client believed that a test conducted on a living person yielded a more accurate assessment of the cutting capacity of a blade than could be had on a dead body.

Yamada preferred to perform cutting tests on the corpses of men whom he had personally executed. The number of corpses he might cut simultaneously for any given test ranged between one and four, depending on the request. The most common request was to cut completely through the chest from one side to the other, just above the nipples, because, as the hardest part of the human body, this was the most difficult to sever. Known in the vernacular as "chopping the breast," this cutting test was usually performed on a single corpse. When cutting two corpses in half with a single stroke, the area across the solar plexus was more suitable.

Two headless corpses, washed of blood, would be brought to the cutting test area, adjacent to the execution grounds. They would be placed beside a mound-shaped platform of firmly packed earth and sand, about one foot in height. The base of the platform would be about two feet in length, twice as long as the flat, rectangular top surface. Four bamboo stakes would be inserted along one edge at the top of the platform. One of the corpses would be laid sideways with its arms extended outward beyond the shoulders, its back against the four stakes at points just below the knees, at the waist, the shoulders and the wrists. The second corpse would be laid out in the same position, with its back flush against the abdomen of the other. The feet and arms of the two corpses would be extended in the same direction, so that the solar plexus of one would be aligned with the other. Four more bamboo stakes would now be driven into the other edge of the platform at positions corresponding to the four stakes on the opposite side, forming a wedge to hold the bodies in place. A rope would then be tied around each pair of bamboo stakes at the top and bottom, to further secure the corpses.

In the hot summer months flies were always a nuisance. They would gather on the exposed stumps of the necks, from which a thin, pink fluid constantly oozed, and swarm around the faces of the corpse handlers. Ignoring the putrid stench of the corpses which he had only one or two hours earlier seen alive, Yamada would draw the blade, and with one clean stroke cut through both bodies at the solar plexus, and into the firmly packed mound of earth and sand below. "Yamada could cut right through ribs, even with a blunt sword," a friend once said. "Unless, of course, his fee was too low." Yamada would take care to strike with the cutting edge, and after making contact, to either push or pull the blade, as if slicing meat with a butcher knife.

Cutting a living person was quite a different matter. This constituted not only a cutting test, but also a brutal form of execution. Yamada's first concern when performing a cutting test on a live body was the object's mental condition. He was relieved to see on this cold, clear morning in late December that his object was not screaming, although his body trembled violently under its fetters. A cutting test, especially on a live person, required great mental composure and tremendous concentration. A display of hysterics by the object might have interfered with Yamada's mental composure, and made concentration difficult. Yamada saw that the prisoner was lean. On a lean body there was a minimal layer of flesh to be penetrated before the blade would come into contact with the rib cage, which presented the sword-tester with his greatest challenge in this particular test. Fatty tissue, however, was easier to cut through than sinews and muscle, while muscular tissue would emit a more explosive gush of blood so that the sword-tester must take care to avoid being covered by the gore. Yamada's final concern was to be careful not to damage the valuable liver when he would cut diagonally across the prisoner's torso.

The rope around the prisoner's right arm was now removed. His body was immediately tied to the wooden post by the upper portion of his right arm, his waist, and ankles. Next his left arm was freed momentarily, before being extended along and tied to the bamboo pole which was parallel to the ground. The top half of his skull was now tied to the uppermost portion of his left arm, so that the base of the backside of his skull touched his left shoulder. The prisoner had been sentenced to die for the murder of a harlot just two days before. Under normal circumstances, even though the prisoner was a lowly commoner, he would have had the benefit of a relatively painless beheading. But the government official who had requested that his sword be tested on a live body was a favorite retainer of a cousin of the Shogun. Had the prisoner been born into the samurai class, even the rampant bribery among Edo officials could not have subjected him to the horror of a cutting test.

Yamada took his place directly in front of the prisoner, bound body and limb to the scaffold. He methodically wrapped his right hand around the hilt then slowly drew the blade, handing the plain wooden sheath to an assistant who stood nearby. As the sword-tester moved his right foot slightly forward, raising the sword above his head with both hands, the condemned man suddenly emitted a hideous scream. To maintain his composure, and concentrate his mental energy at the pit of his abdomen, Yamada released a piercing guttural wail. The morning sunlight reflected off cold steel, revealing the "*beauty of a glowing tempered blade.*" The next instant a stream of blood gushed from the prisoner's body. His torso had been sliced open from the right shoulder to the lower left side, the ribs cut cleanly through and the lungs protruding.

The blade of the influential government official had passed the cutting test. Death was sudden, and the liver remained intact. The sword-tester was satisfied with a job well done. He washed the blade with a ladleful of clear water he took from a nearby pail. After wiping the blade with a piece of soft white paper cloth and handing it to his assistant to resheath, he kneeled over the butchered corpse. With his short sword he made an incision above the navel, then instructed one of the outcasts to remove the liver.*

*Cutting tests and the sale of human liver were banned by the Meiji government in 1870, three years after the fall of the Tokugawa Shogunate. Eleven years later beheading as a form of capital punishment was abolished.

A Natural and Overwhelming Desire

Settings

The Ohmiya (house of a wealthy soy dealer in Kyoto), winter 1867

The Vinegar Store (house of a lumber merchant in Kyoto), winter 1867

The Tenmanya (an inn in Kyoto), winter 1867

Players

Hayashi Kenzo (*L*): A Satsuma samurai

Sakamoto Ryoma (aka Saitani Umetaro) (*L*): A Tosa samurai and revolutionary leader who was assassinated at his hideout in Kyoto

Nakaoka Shintaro (*L*): A Tosa samurai who was assassinated with Ryoma

Miura Kyutaro (*S*): A samurai and elite official of the Kii clan

Sawamura Sonojo (*L*): A follower of Ryoma

Mutsu Yonosuke (*L*): Ryoma's right-hand man

Nakai Shogoro (*L*): A follower of Ryoma and expert swordsman

A Natural and Overwhelming Desire

No human life is replaceable. Death is final. In times of upheaval, however, natural death can be a blessing — to the deceased and to those around him. Death by murder, on the other hand, is sometimes tragic, usually shocking, and most often heartrending. And the murder of a revered leader whose like will never be seen again in the society of men occasionally incites among his bereaved followers a natural and overwhelming desire to wreak vengeance.

It was strikingly cold at early dawn, November 16, 1867, just one month and three days after Shogun Tokugawa Yoshinobu, the supreme ruler of the Japanese nation, had announced his decision to abdicate and restore the Emperor to his ancient seat of power. Hayashi Kenzo, a samurai in the employ of the Satsuma clan, hastened his pace as he walked along a quiet street in the Kawaramachi district of Kyoto, near the headquarters of Tosa and Satsuma. The street was lined with quaint wooden houses with black tile roofs. The shutters behind their latticed windows were closed tightly to keep out the cold wind which blew in from the north, and the lurking danger that had for these past several years turned the once tranquil Imperial capital into a bloodbath of political assassination and murder.

Hayashi had ample reason to hurry. He was cold and tired after his long journey by riverboat from the mercantile capital of Osaka. He was also anxious to meet the man most responsible for the overthrow of the Tokugawa Shogunate. This man was Sakamoto Ryoma, alias Saitani Umetaro, a revolutionary leader and head of a private navy and shipping company who had invited Hayashi to discuss plans for the development of the far northern region of Japan. Ryoma had informed Hayashi of his most recent hideout — a second-story room at the rear of the house of a wealthy soy dealer known as the Ohmiya. Ryoma had been obliged to take the precautions of alias and hideout to elude oppositionists bent on killing the man they blamed most for the overthrow of their supreme leader.

Telltale that these precautions failed horribly were the blood-stained footsteps on the stairway leading from the second story of the Ohmiya, which Hayashi now raced up, only to find Ryoma's corpse lying in a pool of blood, gray matter still oozing from a gaping wound on the forehead, his drawn sword covered by the gore. In the next room Hayashi found the murdered leader's compatriot, Nakaoka Shintaro, mortally wounded but conscious. Downstairs Ryoma's manservant and bodyguard, the former sumo wrestler Tokichi, lay moaning in agony, more dead than alive.

*   *   *

The pale sunlight filtered through the latticed windows of a tatami room on the second floor of an inn in the Gion pleasure quarter of Kyoto. An elite official of the Kii clan, Miura Kyutaro, was seething with anger on this unseasonably cold afternoon in early November 1867. He had just heard from an informer that the man who called himself Saitani Umetaro, commander of the Kaientai, was in reality the notorious outlaw Sakamoto Ryoma, one of the most wanted men on the Shogunate's long list of political enemies. The Kaientai was the private navy and shipping firm which Ryoma had established earlier in the year to run guns for the revolutionaries plotting the overthrow of the government, and to wage war against forces loyal to the Bakufu.

"You're absolutely sure it was Sakamoto who manipulated Minister Goto to convince the Lord of Tosa to write the memorial to His Highness?" Miura confirmed with the informer, his eyes radiating pure hatred for the man who was most responsible for forcing the Shogun to abdicate. Minister Goto was the chief advisor of the influential Lord of Tosa, who, at Goto's urging, had recently petitioned the Shogun to restore Imperial rule over the Japanese nation. The restoration to power of the Emperor meant the fall of the Tokugawa Shogunate, and consequently the demise of the Lord of Kii, whose descendants for two and a half centuries had served the Bakufu as the highest ranking among the elite Three Tokugawa Branch Houses.

But Miura had other, equally compelling reasons to hate Ryoma. In the previous April a steamer of Kii had accidentally rammed and sunk a Kaientai ship. The Kii men were unaware at the time that Ryoma's ship was carrying contraband of four hundred rifles for the revolutionary forces preparing for war against the Shogunate. Nor did they realize that Ryoma had recently armed himself with an even more formidable weapon than these rifles. Ryoma's new weapon was a book on international law, which included maritime law, a subject most Japanese, including the men of Kii, were ignorant. Having lost his ship and cargo due to the incompetence of the Kii sailors, Ryoma demanded monetary compensation from that clan. When Kii refused, he prepared for the first court trial in Japanese history to be conducted, as he now boasted to friends and enemies alike, "in accordance to international law."

Like most samurai, Miura disdained the notion of international law in Japan. "International law is for the damn foreigners," he had snarled upon hearing of Ryoma's intentions. "As a samurai in the service of the Lord of Kii, my only concern is with the laws of the Tokugawa Bakufu and the great domain of Kii."

Meanwhile, Ryoma had concluded that getting public opinion on his side would be vital to the success of his legal battle against as powerful an opponent as Kii. Much to the distress of the Kii men, he contrived a short jingle ridiculing their clan, which he introduced at the brothels of the international port city of Nagasaki, where his company headquarters were located and where influential men from throughout Japan were gathered. Soon harlots and patrons alike were singing the two stanzas which would make Kii the laughing stock of the entire city:

133

It won't be only money we take
for sinking our ship at sea.
We won't give up until we've taken
the entire domain of Kii.

"It won't be only money we take
for sinking our ship at sea.
We won't give up until we've taken
the heads of all the men of Kii.

In May, Kii offered to pay an indemnity in the enormous sum of 83,000 gold *ryo* if Ryoma would agree to drop the case. The outlaw had taken on the highest-ranking feudal clan in Japan, and the outlaw had won. And now, Miura Kyutaro was consumed with hate for the man who, in October, would overthrow the government.

*   *   *

The cold night air penetrated the wooden walls of the house of the lumber merchant known curiously as the "Vinegar Store," located on a narrow back street in the Kawaramachi district of Kyoto, just west of the Sanjo Bridge which traversed the Takasegawa canal. The Vinegar Store had been the hideout of Sakamoto Ryoma, until he had recently made the ill-fated move to the nearby shop of the wealthy soy dealer. A group of six men who now called themselves the "Executive Committee" had secretly gathered at the Vinegar Store on the grim night of November eighteenth. Earlier in the day they had been among a larger group of men who had escorted the coffins of their slain leader and the two others to the cemetery of a Buddhist temple in the green mountains on the east side of the Imperial capital. Filled with grief, and burning with a natural and overwhelming desire to wreak vengeance, the men of the Executive Committee now spoke passionately, deliberately laying their plan of attack.

134

The assassins had left behind two items — an empty scabbard and a pair of wooden clogs — which led Ryoma's men to believe that they were members of the Shinsengumi, a police corps of expert swordsmen with a vendetta against the revolutionary leader. The scabbard was identified by a defector of the Shinsengumi as that of one Harada Sanosuke, a member of the corps. Harada hailed from the province of Iyo, on the island of Shikoku, which bordered Ryoma's and Nakaoka's native Tosa. It had been reported by Nakaoka before his death two days after the attack that one of the assailants had screamed a profanity in the Iyo dialect. Furthermore, the wooden clogs left behind were identified as those belonging to a nearby inn, from the mark of that inn engraved in the wood. When the clogs were presented to a maid at the inn on the day after the attack, she testified that the night before she had lent the clogs to one of a group of seven men who had identified themselves as members of the Shinsengumi.

"We know it was them," seethed Sawamura Sonojo, a close personal friend and follower of the murdered leader.

"We must kill Harada to revenge Commander Sakamoto's death," said another man.

"But there were others beside Harada involved," insisted Mutsu Yonosuke, who had served as Ryoma's right-hand man for these past several years.

"Then we must kill them all," exploded Sonojo.

"Yes, let's kill each and every one of the bastards," hollered another man, whose sentiments were echoed by several others.

"We must remain calm," Yonosuke said. "Commander Sakamoto would demand nothing less."

"How can we be calm until we've gotten vengeance on ..."

"First we must kill their ringleader," Yonosuke interrupted, before adding bitterly, "a high-ranking Kii official by the name of Miura Kyutaro."

Over the days following, the six men of the Executive Committee kept a constant watch on the comings and goings of

Miura, but the opportunity for attack did not readily afford itself. In time they discovered that Miura frequented a certain house of pleasure, located in the Gion quarter. They also found out that Miura was fond of a certain young girl, who was in the employ of that house. On the night of December sixth, they received word that Miura was at his favorite pleasure house with the girl. Soon six two-sworded men, each armed with a pistol, lay in wait near the front gate of the house.

For the six men bent on vengeance, the cold night passed without incident. Early the next morning a palanquin carrying a man whom they suspected to be Miura departed the premises through the front gate. The six men followed the palanquin through narrow residential streets, then northward along the western bank of the Kamogawa. Finally, one of the six bid the palanquin bearers stop, and when they did a voice from within called "Who goes there?" One of them raised the palanquin curtain, revealing a lone samurai, who grasped tightly the shark-skin-bound hilt of his short sword in one hand and who was certainly not Miura Kyutaro. "What's the meaning of this?" he demanded.

"Did you not drink *sake* with Miura last night?" asked one of the six.

"I did. But Miura left at midnight."

The men of the Executive Committee were perplexed. "How could we have let him escape?" they asked each other upon their return to the Vinegar Store. "We were watching for him the entire night." They soon, however, realized that they had only let Miura escape after being duped by the lone samurai in the palanquin who grasped tightly his short sword.

*   *   *

The dead of the Kyoto winter was upon them, as the men of the Executive Committee, and ten others, sat huddled around a small cask of *sake*, in a room at the Vinegar Store on the night of December seventh.

"We know for a fact that Miura is at the Tenmanya tonight," Yonosuke said, referring to an inn which he had seen Miura enter that evening.

"We must make a farewell toast before we leave to carry out our final task," one of them said, because all were prepared to die avenging their leader's murder. Each man in turn drained a ladleful of clear *sake*, uttering his vow of vengeance as he drank.

"We don't know how many of the enemy will be with Miura," Yonosuke said. "But we must not let him escape this time. We will split up into three groups. Seven of us will enter the inn through the front door. Although we won't know which room Miura is in, we must catch him off guard, without any prior warning. And so we must remain calm and nonchalant, as if we had come to visit Miura. I will present a fake calling card, identifying myself with an alias. Six of you will remain outside to cut Miura in case he should try to escape through the front door. The remaining three will guard the back exit. Then, once we know where Miura is, we must attack immediately."

"One shot by any of us," said Sonojo, drawing a revolver from his jacket, "will be a signal to the others that Miura has been killed. At that point, those who are still alive should escape immediately."

A heavy snow was falling when the sixteen men arrived at the Tenmanya inn at ten o'clock that night. According to plan, Yonosuke and six others entered through the front door. Among them was a bearded youth of only twenty years by the name of Nakai Shogoro. Nakai, who had earlier in the year single-handedly cut down two swordsmen of the Shinsengumi, was exceptionally skilled at the lethal art of drawing a sword, but short on patience. At his left hip he wore a sword given him that summer by Sakamoto Ryoma, and inscribed with his name near the guard, just above the hilt. "I'll give my life for Ryoma," he had vowed. Without waiting for Yonosuke to present the fake calling card, Nakai dashed up the wooden stairway, and down a dark corridor on the second floor. He heard voices behind a closed door, which he threw open, revealing a small gathering, consisting of Miura and twelve other samurai, each sitting at a small, low table set with *sake* cup and flask. In the light of several lanterns, Nakai surmised that two of these men were of the Aizu clan, the others members of the Shinsengumi who had been assigned as bodyguards to Miura. Nakai moved directly in front of Miura, drew his razor-sharp blade from its scabbard, and in the same motion struck his enemy about the face. In his eagerness to kill, Nakai merely grazed Miura, as pandemonium ensued. Yonosuke and the others burst into the room with swords drawn. The enemy met drawn sword with drawn sword, and amidst the chaos the lanterns went out. Blood sprayed in the darkness, steel crashed against steel, the guttural wailing of men killing and being killed filled the room and echoed through the house. Then a voice falsely claimed "I've killed Miura," a single gunshot rang out, and fifteen men escaped into the cold Kyoto night.

The Attack at the Tenmanya left four men of the former Shogunate wounded, and four of them dead. Miura Kyutaro, having escaped by climbing through a window and onto the roof, had only been slightly wounded about the face. Of the men bent on avenging Ryoma's murder, only Nakai was killed. He had fought fiercely, killing or wounding several of the enemy before his own sword snapped in two, rendering him defenseless.

At first thought it would seem that Yonosuke and his men had again been duped. But on certain fortuitous occasions fate employs strange means of righting a wrong, or as the case may be, of allowing men to inadvertently avoid tragedy. Two years later, in a deposition at the Ministry of Penal Affairs, an expert swordsman by the name of Imai Nobuo testified that the assassins were not men of the Shinsengumi, but rather of another

Tokugawa police unit known as the Patrolling Corps, and that he and six others had committed the murders. Imai's testimony all but exonerated Miura of masterminding the assassination of Sakamoto Ryoma.

Discipline

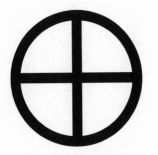

DISCIPLINE

Setting

A training hall in Kagoshima Castletown, February 1868

Players

Unnamed samurai youths of the Satsuma clan

Discipline

Just as resolve to die in the service of one's lord was a paragon of samurai virtue, strength of mind and fortitude of spirit were perhaps the most essential qualities of the warrior. These rudiments of true courage, only obtained through great difficulty, were most often forged through severe martial training. Perhaps the most severe of all samurai training, mentally and physically, was that practiced by the warriors of the Satsuma clan, whose martial traditions had been unparalleled for centuries.

The code of conduct for the Satsuma samurai was the strictest in all Japan. As a boy he was not just a member of his immediate family, but a treasure of his clan. He would grow up to serve his liege lord, and was merely entrusted to his family until then. He was treated with special deference by his mother and sisters, and kept separated from girls to ensure that his virility would not be tainted. In a culture where the expression "revere men, scorn women" was deeply embedded in the social mores, it was not uncommon for a mother to wash the clothes of her husband and sons separately from her daughters' and her own. At the age of five, the samurai boy was invested in the traditional garb of the warrior — a kimono displaying his family crest, pleated trousers, and two swords stuck in his sash at his left hip. Thus adorned, his long black hair oiled and tied in a neat topknot, he was brought to pray at the ancestral grave site, and subsequently enrolled at the local martial brotherhood. Here he would begin twenty years of rigorous discipline in the forms of scholastic studies and martial arts training. His academic pursuits consisted of calligraphy, memorization of the classical poetry of Satsuma, a thorough reading of the Satsuma war chronicles, and later the Chinese classics. The Satsuma samurai was trained in a particularly lethal style of kenjutsu, which emphasized killing an opponent with a single blow. Younger boys practiced with a hard, oak sword. Advanced students wielded real blades on the corpses of executed criminals, to experience the sensation of cutting human flesh, and to test a sword's capacity to do so.

Upon a February evening in the year 1868, twelve youths gathered in a training hall in Kagoshima Castletown, the capital of Satsuma. The dark wood paneled room was cold, but the youths wore only light cotton robes and trousers. They were barefoot, and sat cross-legged in a circle on the polished wooden floor. At the center of the circle hung a loaded musket, fastened to the end of a rope which was suspended from a wooden rafter.

The young men were drinking potent white liquor from a gourd jug. They talked about the coming war that over these past several months had become the single most important thing for them, for the great domain of Satsuma and indeed for all of Japan. As they talked they passed the jug around the circle, and the more they drank the more heatedly they spoke.

One of the youths now stood up and lit the matchlock on the musket. He took hold of the butt and spun the gun clockwise, then quickly resumed his place in the circle. As the matchlock burned down to the pan, the muzzle alternately pointed at each of them, so that the loaded gun might fire into any of their faces at any time. But their purpose this evening was to train themselves to overcome fear in wartime, regardless of impending danger. The loser was not the one who was the first to be wounded, or, as the case may be, killed, but rather he who was first to prostrate himself in the face of the lethal lead ball.

War was imminent. The Imperial forces, led by Satsuma and Choshu, had been raring to crush the Tokugawa since the previous summer. The stage for bloody revolution had been set. The leaders of the new government had received orders from the Imperial Court to strike. But war had been averted in the eleventh hour, when, on October fourteenth, the last Shogun, Tokugawa Yoshinobu, had announced his momentous decision in Kyoto. The Shogun had agreed to relinquish his family's centuries-long rule and restore power to the Emperor. However, the

Aizu and Kuwana clans, with other die-hard Tokugawa supporters, including the Shinsengumi, refused to follow
Yoshinobu's example. Rather, they prepared for a final show-
down with the forces of the new Imperial government, whom
they disdained, even now, as renegades.

In command of the Imperial forces was Saigo Kichinosuke,
the great Satsuma leader whom every samurai youth in Satsuma
revered as a hero. And although they were not yet old enough to
fight alongside their elder brothers and fathers, most of whom
were now stationed with Saigo in the Osaka-Kyoto region, they
longed for the day when such honor would be theirs. "We will
have no cowards among us," they repeatedly vowed. "We must
prepare ourselves to die courageously in battle," they told one
another, and it was through rigorous training in the way of the
sword, and games to test their nerve with loaded guns, that they
would.

Like so many customs of man, the Satsuma youths' game of
daring, for all its virtues, was not without its flaws. The nerves
of the players were unnaturally calm from the liquor they had
consumed this evening. A player whose physical constitution
prevented his consumption of alcohol would certainly be at a
disadvantage. His nerves, naturally more taut than his comrades, would tend to interfere with his will to brave death. And
as it happened, there was just such a youth in the circle on this
particular evening. Try as he would to ignore the danger of the
spinning gun, the matchlock burning fast, he could not suppress
his instinct for survival. Unbearably long were the ensuing several seconds before the matchlock burned down to the pan and
the musket finally fired its lethal charge. The faces of those
around him, flush with liquor, filled him with unspeakable
dread. He agonized over the shame he would cause his family,
and the humiliation he would surely suffer for the rest of his
life. He judged himself unworthy of his status as a Satsuma
samurai. Certainly he would never again wear his two swords
with the dignity of a brave warrior. Certainly he would never

have the honor of fighting alongside his father and elder brothers in the war against Aizu and Kuwana. Nor did he deserve the privilege of inheriting his family's line, in case his father and brothers should perish in battle. The youth determined to leave the Satsuma clan, to live alone, without family or friends, in exile in the southern islands. He thought about all of these things and more, in only a matter of seconds. Then suddenly he threw himself facedown on the floor, a loud explosion filled his head, and in the next instant he was overcome with a deadening remorse.

One week elapsed. The disgraced youth was now determined to redeem his honor and that of his family's, or else fulfill his self-sworn vow of exile. He reported to the same training hall at the same hour as he had during the previous week. He took his place in the same circle of his peers whose flush faces had constantly remained in his mind over these past seven days. The same musket hung from the same rope, suspended from the same rafter. The gourd jug of potent white liquor was passed around, but try as he might to indulge, the mere smell of alcohol made him sick. Presently someone lit the matchlock, took hold of the butt and spun the musket. The muzzle now pointed alternately in the direction of each of the twelve youths. When the matchlock had burnt halfway down to the pan, the disgraced youth was suddenly overcome with a feeling of calm such as he had never before known, as if his suffering of the past week was more soporific to the nerves than the white liquor of his peers. When the matchlock had burnt three-quarters of the way down to the pan, he was filled with the ecstasy of epiphany. He felt as if he had discovered absolute courage in the face of glaring death. The next instant there was a loud explosion, the lethal lead ball crashed into his forehead, and the young man, redeemed of precious honor, fell dead.

"Serene As the Sky, and Open As the Sea"

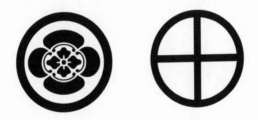

"SERENE AS THE SKY, AND OPEN AS THE SEA"

Settings

A spacious tatami room at Satsuma's estate in Edo, March 1868

A place just beyond the main gate of Satsuma's estate in Edo, March 1868

Players

Katsu Kaishu (*S*): Head of the Tokugawa Army, vice-commissioner of the Tokugawa Navy, a loyal retainer of the former Shogun, and the most powerful man in Edo

Saigo Kichinosuke (*L*): A Satsuma samurai, and commander-in-chief of the forces of the new Imperial government

"Serene as the Sky, and Open as the Sea"

Would the new rulers of the Japanese nation unleash fifty thou-sand Imperial troops upon the capital of the former Shogun? Or would the Tokugawa samurai who had taken it upon himself to save his native Edo from the torch succeed in persuading the enemy commander to spare the life and lineage of his liege lord? "Let me tell you something about Saigo's magnanimity," the samurai would address the matter in retrospect. "With the Imperial forces set to advance into the city and attack Edo Castle, all it took was one letter from me and he came at his own leisurely pace to talk at the Satsuma estate."

Such were the words of former Tokugawa Navy Commissioner Katsu Kaishu about Saigo Kichinosuke of Satsuma, a giant of a man also known as "Saigo the Great," the quintessential samu-rai who cherished the words *"Love mankind, revere heaven,"* and who in March 1868 was, for all means and purposes, the commander-in-chief of the Imperial forces bent on crushing the remnants of the Tokugawa Shogunate.

In the previous October, the last Shogun, Tokugawa Yoshinobu, had announced his abdication and the restoration of power to the Emperor. Yoshinobu's good intentions for a blood-less revolution notwithstanding, two and a half centuries of Tokugawa rule would not end so easily. Oppositionists, particu-larly the samurai of the powerful Aizu and Kuwana clans, were disgusted with the Shogun's peaceful abdication. They were determined to defend what they felt was their rightful rule, just as the samurai of Satsuma and Choshu, whose leaders com-manded the Imperial forces, were determined to annihilate the Tokugawa to ensure that it would never rise again.

War finally broke out just south of Kyoto on January third. When reports of the first artillery fire reached Saigo at his near-by headquarters, his eyes lit up like sparkling black diamonds on his large, corpulent face, and he said to his *aides-de-camp,*

"The sound of a single cannon shot makes me happier than if we had obtained another one million troops."

For all his elation, the commander-in-chief was deeply worried. While the combined Imperial forces throughout Japan totaled fifty thousand strong, those in Kyoto were outnumbered more than threefold by the troops of the Tokugawa. But when Saigo proceeded to the battlefield his mind was immediately set at ease. His 4,500 troops had forced 15,000 of the enemy to retreat, in what would end three days later in a rout by the Imperial forces.

Yoshinobu, to display his absolute allegiance to the new Imperial government, not to mention to its leaders who were faithful adherents in the belief that "revolution is born from the barrel of a gun," had vacated his stronghold of Edo Castle in February. The new leaders, however, would not be readily placated. They demanded that the former Shogun commit *seppuku*, and set March fifteenth as the date fifty thousand Imperial troops would lay siege to Edo Castle, and in so doing subject the entire city to the flames of war.

In March 1868, Katsu Kaishu was the most powerful man in Edo. As Vice-commissioner of the Tokugawa Navy, he had a formidable fleet of twelve warships at his command. As head of the Tokugawa Army, he was resolved to burn Edo Castle rather than relinquish it to the enemy, and to wage a bloody war against the Imperial forces. Although Katsu desperately wanted to avoid a civil war, which he feared might end in foreign subjugation, he was bound by his duty as a direct retainer of the Tokugawa to serve in the best interest of his liege lord, Tokugawa Yoshinobu.* When Katsu was informed of the new government's plans for an imminent attack on Edo, he immediately sent a letter to Saigo at general headquarters, just a two-day journey west of Edo. In this letter Katsu made no mention

---

*Although no longer Shogun, Yoshinobu was still Head of the House of Tokugawa.

of his determination that the new government must treat the Tokugawa and the former Shogun with leniency. Rather, he pointed out that the retainers of the Tokugawa were an inseparable part of the new Japanese nation. Instead of fighting with one another, those of the new regime and the old must cooperate in order to deal with the very real threat of the foreign powers, whose legations in Japan anxiously watched the great revolution which had consumed the Japanese nation for these past fifteen years.

Saigo replied immediately with a set of conditions, including the surrender of Edo Castle, which must be met if the House of Tokugawa was to be allowed to survive, Yoshinobu's life spared, and war avoided. The historic meeting between Katsu and Saigo, which determined the fate of the city of Edo and the future of Japan, was now set for March fourteenth, five months after Yoshinobu had announced his abdication, and one day before the Imperial forces would attack.

No one more than Saigo sympathized with Katsu's loyalty to his liege lord. Saigo was born in Kagoshima Castletown in 1827, the eldest son of an impoverished petty samurai. In 1851 a new *daimyo* came to power in Satsuma. His name was Shimazu Nariakira, and he would not only change the life of Saigo Kichinosuke, but indeed the history of Japan. Lord Nariakira was a radical reformer who, with the coming of Perry in 1853, realized that Japan must modernize itself through Western technology to avoid foreign subjugation. He fortified the coastal defenses of Satsuma. He planted mines in the sea approaches to Kagoshima Castletown. (It was only by luck that the British ships would avoid these mines during their bombardment of Kagoshima in 1863.) He convinced the Shogunate to abolish its ban on the building of large ships, and subsequently produced a Western-style sailing vessel which became the first to fly the banner of the Rising Sun. He constructed Western-style factories and a reverberatory furnace for the manufacture of warships, cannon, rifles and other advanced weaponry. In 1854, only fifteen years after the invention of photography in Europe, Nariakira took the first photographs in Japan with a camera he built himself. In 1858, just twelve years after the introduction of telegraphy in Europe, this most innovative of Japanese feudal lords set up a simple telegraph system within the precincts of his castle. The farsighted *daimyo* was constantly on the lookout for promising young men among his vassals. Fortunately for Satsuma, and the Japanese nation, he was wise enough to recognize ability among the lower echelons of the samurai class. In 1854, Nariakira chose Saigo, an obscure official, to accompany him on his first attendance at Edo as Lord of Satsuma.

Nariakira never regretted his choice. One day in Edo, while discussing the situation in Satsuma with an elite shogunal councilor, Nariakira demonstrated his ability to recognize genius. "Although the House of Shimazu has a great many vassals," he told the councilor, "unfortunately there is only one among them whom we can depend upon in such difficult times as these. His name is Saigo. Please remember the name, because he's the greatest treasure we have in Satsuma."

After four years of faithful service under Nariakira, Saigo was crushed by the sudden death of his lord. He determined to die by his own sword, because *seppuku* was the ultimate display of loyalty by a samurai to his liege lord. Saigo only abandoned his plan when a friend convinced him of his duty to carry on Nariakira's legacy by strengthening Japan. This Saigo did, emerging in 1864 as the most powerful man in Satsuma and a key player in the epoch drama which was the overthrow of the Tokugawa dynasty. Now, four years later, in a spacious tatami room at the official Satsuma estate in Edo, Saigo, as commander-in-chief of the Imperial forces, would meet with Katsu Kaishu, the most powerful man of the Tokugawa camp and the only one among them whom he fully trusted.

"What particularly impressed me about Saigo," Count Katsu* would recall shortly before his death in 1899, "was that he treated me with the respect due a chief retainer of the Tokugawa, and that throughout our discussion he maintained a formal posture, his hands on his lap, without exercising his authority as the victor to look down upon a commander of the defeated side. In his great courage, he was serene as the sky, and open as the sea."

The two men had first met four years before, in the fall of 1864, shortly after Katsu had sent his right-hand man, Sakamoto Ryoma, to meet Saigo at the Satsuma estate in Kyoto, and just before being dismissed as navy commissioner and placed under house arrest for harboring known renegades at his private naval academy in Kobe. "The first time I met Saigo," Katsu reminisced, "was at an inn in Osaka. Dressed in a black crepe jacket displaying the Saigo family crest of a horse's bridle, he was quite an imposing figure." Imposing indeed! At nearly six feet tall and over 240 pounds, Saigo was almost twice the size of Katsu, who was less than five feet high and of a slender, wiry build. "Saigo," Katsu once said, "was one of the two most frightening men I have ever met."

Katsu, for his part, impressed Saigo with no less impact. The commissioner of the Tokugawa Navy was a visionary who recognized several years before the fall of the Shogunate the inevitability of its collapse. During their first meeting, Katsu pressed upon Saigo the urgent necessity for the most powerful samurai clans, including Satsuma, to cooperate with one another to form a new government. Saigo expressed his admiration for the navy commissioner in a letter to a compatriot in Satsuma: "*I met Katsu for the first time. He is certainly an amazing man. Although I had at first intended to strike him down, I soon bowed my head to him in reverence.*"

Now, after four years of unprecedented turmoil in Japan, Saigo again bowed his head upon entering the spacious tatami room at the Satsuma estate in Edo, where Katsu was waiting for

*Katsu Kaishu was created count in 1887.

him. "Excuse me for being late," Saigo said.

"I had come on horseback that day, with only one attendant," Katsu recalled of the meeting in March 1868. "Saigo was wearing European-style clothes and the wooden clogs of Satsuma. He entered the room from the garden, a casual look on his face, and not as if he were confronted with the important business at hand."

Certainly Saigo was thinking similar thoughts about Katsu, who began speaking easily, in a slick downtown Edo accent, and not as if the very fate of the great city rested upon his shoulders. "Saigo-san, you and I well know that we must never let ourselves be complacent in our victories, or overwhelmed by our defeats." Katsu wore his thick, black hair tied in a topknot. He was dressed formally in a black silk jacket, on which was displayed the Katsu family crest of a four-petaled flower in a circle.

"Of course not," Saigo said, nodding heavily his large head, his black diamond eyes radiating pure sincerity and nothing else, as he waited for Katsu to continue.

"The urgency of the situation we are faced with demands nothing less." Katsu was silenced by the sudden boom of artillery fire, which shook the thin walls of the wooden Satsuma estate, and immediately brought a smile to Saigo's face.

"Never mind, Katsu-sensei," the great man said. "Just some of our troops getting prepared."

"I see," Katsu said, snickering. "After the beating they gave our forces in Kyoto, I trust they are already prepared."

"Yes, they are," Saigo replied, taking Katsu's ironic banter seriously.

"The reality is," Katsu said, the humor now gone from his voice, "both your side, who are the victor, and our side, who are the defeated, must look beyond the narrow scope of individual clan, the House of Tokugawa, or even the Imperial Court." Katsu paused momentarily, as if to give Saigo a chance to speak, but the large man simply nodded agreement. "We must cooperate with one another, Saigo-san, and consider the overall interest of Japan first and foremost, or both of our sides will perish."

"I see," Saigo said, staring hard into Katsu's eyes and asking gravely, "But can you convince Aizu and Kuwana of the same?"

"I must," Katsu asserted.

"Yes, you must," Saigo agreed, still looking hard at his adversary. "But how?"

"By pressing upon them the reality that the French for certain, and the British perhaps, are eagerly waiting for civil war to break out between us, so that they may seize the opportunity to subjugate and colonize Japan when we are at our weakest."

Saigo smiled sadly, dropping his eyes. "You sound like Sakamoto-san," he said, alluding to Katsu's former disciple who two years earlier had convinced the bitter enemies of Satsuma and Choshu to unite with one another as the first giant step toward sealing the fate of the Tokugawa.

"That's because Ryoma learned everything he knew from me," Katsu said, laughing aloud and drawing a blank look from Saigo. "But enough of that," he said, producing a document from his breast pocket, then handing it to the Satsuma man.

"Saigo treated me with perfect trust," Katsu recalled of the historic meeting, during which he agreed with the conditions previously put forth by the Imperial government.

"I will have to discuss things at general headquarters," Saigo said. "But I guarantee with my life to abide by everything we have decided upon here today."

"With this one word from Saigo," Katsu recalled, "the lives and property of Edo's one million occupants were spared, and the House of Tokugawa was saved from destruction. Had it been anyone other than Saigo, that person would have censured us for all sorts of things, and our negotiations would have certainly collapsed."

With the discussion concluded, Saigo escorted Katsu just beyond the main gate of the Satsuma estate. Outside the estate a unit of Imperial troops armed with rifles were suddenly upon Katsu. But they must have seen their commander-in-chief escort the Tokugawa official to the gate, because no sooner did they spot Katsu than did the entire unit raise their rifles in salute.

Katsu remained where he stood, facing the enemy troops. "You'd better take a good look," he said, pointing at his own chest. "Depending on what is decided in the next day or two, you might have to shoot me."

Katsu's formidable courage notwithstanding, he was well aware upon taking his leave of Saigo that he would not be killed by Imperial troops, just as he knew that the siege on Edo Castle which was planned for the following day would never be, and that the Tokugawa stronghold of two and a half centuries would be peacefully surrendered to the Imperial government shortly after.

Disgrace

Settings

A scene of military confrontation, near the left bank of the Edogawa river, a half day's journey on horseback west of Edo, April 1868

A camp of the Imperial forces, not far from the mentioned scene of military confrontation

An open field at Imperial headquarters in the Itabashi district of Edo, April 1868

Players

Arima Tota (*L*): A Satsuma samurai, and vice-chief of staff of the Imperial Army

Kondo Isami (aka Okubo Yamato) (*S*): Former commander of the Shinsengumi (a shogunal police corps)

Disgrace

It was honor redeemed for a samurai who, sentenced to die, was permitted the dignity of disembowelment by his own sword. Beheading and other means of execution, the fate of common criminals, were the utmost disgrace to the men who lived and died by the code of the warrior. Even a truly valiant man, however, vanquished in battle and taken captive, was not readily afforded the honor of seppuku — arming him with the necessary blade presented too great a danger to his captors. More often than not the prisoner of war was put to the ignominy of the executioner's sword. To assure the absolute destruction of the fallen enemy, both in life and death, his severed head might then be mounted atop a bamboo stake stuck in the soft mud along a river, and left to the ravages of the elements, birds of prey and the derision of the vulgar masses.

The red glow of dawn dominated the land with no more authority than the Imperial banner — a sixteen-petaled chrysanthemum emblazoned in gold against brilliant vermilion — waving in the wind above a unit of three hundred Imperial troops armed with rifles and swords. Some wore military uniforms of the English style, others traditional kimono and pleated trousers, as they marched into the village of Nagare-yama, on the left bank of the Edogawa river, in the province of Shimo-usa, a half day's journey on horseback west of Edo. In the previous month, March 1868, Tokugawa emissary Katsu Kaishu had spared the former Shogun's capital from the torch by agreeing with Saigo Kichinosuke, commander of the Imperial forces, to peacefully relinquish Edo Castle to the Imperial government. While the government prepared to occupy the fortress, it set itself to the task of eliminating the oppositionist forces who refused to accept their own fate and that of their liege lord, the last Tokugawa Shogun.

As the Imperial troops of Vice-chief of Staff Arima Tota of

Satsuma surrounded Nagare-yama, they were greeted by the staccato of gunfire from one hundred twenty samurai. Arima's mission on this balmy spring morning was to arrest the leader of these samurai, whom he suspected to be Kondo Isami, commander of the Shinsengumi, the former Shogun's most dreaded police corps.

Suddenly the crackling of the rifles ceased, and from the enemy side appeared two samurai brandishing drawn swords, flanking a third man, his long and short swords sheathed at his left hip, whom they escorted forward, slowly but steadily, as if oblivious to the three hundred guns trained on them by men whose comrades they had butchered by the score over these past several years of bloody revolution. The three men drew nearer, but still Arima did not issue the command to fire. Now the two escorts sheathed their blades, as all three continued their advance with the perfect decorum of valiant samurai, stopping right before the Imperial officer.

"Who are you?" Arima demanded.

The samurai at the center of the line presented a calling card, identifying himself as Okubo Yamato, the alias Kondo had assumed to evade arrest by the new government, upon his elevation to the rank of councilor to the former Shogun. Kondo did not know, however, that recently his alias had been disclosed by government agents.

"We exchanged fire with you this morning," Kondo said solemnly, the severity in his eyes complemented by an unusually large mouth, heavy jaw and full head of thick, black hair tied in a topknot, striking Arima as the demeanor of a true warrior, and the description he had heard of the notorious swordsman. "But only when we saw the Chrysanthemum standard did we realize that you were troops of the Imperial government."

"I see," said Arima, taken aback by the firm resolve to die which emanated from Kondo's calm bearing. "We will have to ask you to relinquish your artillery and return with us to our camp at Kasukabe for questioning." So impressed, however,

was Arima with the noble mien of this direct retainer of the former Shogun, that he readily accepted his promise to report to
the nearby camp with the artillery in hand.

Arima led his troops back to their camp at Kasukabe to await
Kondo's arrival. At four-thirty the same afternoon three cannon
and three hundred rifles were delivered from Nagare-yama to
the Imperial camp, without any sign, however, of the commander of the Shinsengumi. It was for the purpose of retrieving
the war criminal that the vice-chief of staff himself set out on
horseback, with an escort of only five rank-and-file soldiers.

The banner of vermilion and gold was faintly visible in the dim
light of dusk, waving in the wind above the village of Nagare-
yama, as Arima dismounted his horse.

"When we arrived at Kondo's camp, we were greeted in a
friendly manner by the two samurai who earlier in the day had
escorted their commander, brandishing their drawn swords,"
Arima would report over a half century later, in 1923, by which
time certain episodes from the last days of the samurai had
slipped into that hazy realm which lay between historical fact
and legendary anecdote. The guards were soon followed by
Kondo, who greeted Arima with the same friendly attitude.
Although Kondo clearly had no alternative but to surrender to
the Imperial troops, his display of perfect composure, "without
any look of belligerence on his face," impressed Arima.

Kondo excused himself momentarily. When he returned,
accompanied by two young attendants, he was dressed formally in a black jacket and gray pleated trousers. At his left hip he
wore two swords. "Dignified," Arima would describe the enemy
leader, who now presented the two younger men with a pistol
and a short sword. "As keepsakes," he told his attendants, who
entreated their master to allow them to accompany him to the
Imperial camp. Although Kondo refused their request, on the
grounds that it was "improper," Arima granted them permission
to manifest their loyalty. "Kondo and I both rode on horseback,

with his attendants walking on either side of their master's horse, holding firmly the bit," Arima would recall.

The party did not arrive at the Imperial camp until midnight. When Arima awoke the next morning, he found a single palanquin, covered by a heavy net and set in front of the camp. Arima soon discovered that without his knowledge Kondo had been placed inside the palanquin, by which he would be escorted as a common criminal to Imperial headquarters at Edo's Itabashi district. "He is the leader of an army," Arima roared indignantly to his subordinate who had so insulted the enemy commander. "You simply don't know how to treat a samurai."

Arima now ordered the net removed, and personally saw to it that Kondo was provided with tea, tobacco, a long-stemmed pipe and other accessories to a comfortable journey, but notably refused the swordsman his request to be allowed to keep his two swords.

While the authorities at Imperial headquarters knew that the man who called himself Okubo Yamato was actually Kondo Isami, they lacked proof of their conviction. It just so happened, however, that stationed at headquarters was a former member of Kondo's corps, who had recently defected to the Imperial side, and nearly been killed in a retaliatory attack ordered by Kondo himself. When Kondo's former comrade-in-arms exposed his identify, he readily accepted his fate, and composed a death song in bold, flowing brush strokes of black Chinese ink.

Captured by the enemy,
  I have nothing to say of my past,
  but choose honor over life.

Ah, the long shining sword
  to which I readily surrender,
  and repay my lord's kindness with my life.

*   *   *

The banner of vermilion and gold waved in the radiant blue sky above an empty field bounded on one side by an oak grove on the balmy spring morning of April twenty-fifth. Dressed formally in a kimono of black linen and dark pleated trousers, a white sash around his waist, stood the condemned man. He was barefoot. A slight beard covered his heavy jaw, a dark expression his pallid face. His arms were bound firmly at both sides with heavy rope, wound several times around his torso. Surrounding him were some thirty Imperial guards armed with rifles, one of them on horseback. The field was duly prepared with a freshly dug hole in front of a piece of coarse straw matting, onto which the prisoner now sat with dignity, in the formal position — feet tucked underneath, head up, back straight, hands resting easily on his thighs. He briefly turned his face toward the sky, squinting in the bright sunlight, before returning his dark gaze directly ahead, at the nothingness which awaited him. "I've been a great trouble," he said calmly in a loud, clear voice, without removing his eyes from the empty field.

Whether he was merely humbling himself in vain hope that his life might be spared, or whether he spoke with complete sincerity, it is certain that Kondo Isami had been much more than a great trouble to his enemies over these last five of the thirty-five years of his short, truculent life.

A peasant's son from the province of Musashi, near Edo, Kondo Isami was raised with a training sword in his hand. His father, a great enthusiast of the martial arts, maintained a private *dojo* at his home. Here a fencing instructor from the nearby capital taught Isami and his two elder brothers three times each month. The instructor was master of the Shieikan Fencing Academy, where some sixty students practiced daily in the Tennen Rishin Style. The sword master was getting along in age. He did not have a son, and was impressed with Isami's ferocity on the practice floor. At age fourteen, Isami became the sword master's disciple, at age seventeen his adopted son, and soon after, the fourth generational master of the Tennen Rishin Style. "Although Kondo's fencing technique was not as polished as some of the others," a nephew of Isami's closest comrade would recall sixty years after his death, "he was famous for his great courage."

It was with this great courage, two swords and a determination to make a name for himself as a samurai in the service of the Shogun that Kondo Isami, with several of his top swordsmen, set out from Edo for the distant Imperial capital. This was in the early spring of 1863, during the reign of terror in Kyoto by anti-Bakufu renegades led by the Loyalists of the Choshu and Tosa clans. The Bakufu was making the final preparations for the first visit to Kyoto by a Shogun in over two centuries. In order to suppress the renegades, the Tokugawa authorities would "fight fire with fire." To this purpose, and under the slogan of "loyalty and patriotism," the Bakufu recruited over two hundred *ronin* from provinces around Japan, among them Kondo and his men. Shortly after the "loyal and patriotic corps" reached Kyoto, however, the Bakufu had second thoughts about the wisdom of their plan. It became apparent that many of these *ronin* were actually Imperial Loyalists at heart, and that they shared the xenophobic sentiments of the Choshu and Tosa men whom they had been enlisted to suppress. Most of them were returned to Edo, where they could do little harm. Some twenty of them, however, opted to remain in Kyoto. These men were placed under the supervision of the Lord of Aizu, a staunch Tokugawa ally and the Bakufu's official Protector of Kyoto. The diminished company of *ronin* assumed the name *Shinsengumi,* "Newly Selected Corps," among whom were Kondo and his group of expert swordsmen. Three corps commanders were chosen, Kondo one of them. Differences of opinion ensued, the ranks split into two factions, one led by Kondo, the other by a charismatic but reckless man whose name was Serizawa Kamo.

Serizawa had a reputation as a violent drunk. After he had made too many enemies, the Lord of Aizu secretly ordered Kondo and several others to assassinate him. Kondo carried out these orders with the same cold-blooded expedience by which his corps would subdue the enemies of the Tokugawa. He now became the sole leader of the Shinsengumi, which he and Hijikata Toshizo, his chief confidant and right-hand man, would command with an iron rule.

With the fall of the Tokugawa Shogunate, that iron rule had ended, and Kondo Isami, seated at the scaffold on this balmy spring morning, remained calm. He was suddenly overcome by a sharp pain in his left shoulder, which had been shattered by a sniper's bullet as he rode on horseback in the previous December. Kondo's party of twenty had been ambushed as they traveled southward from Kyoto to the nearby town of Fushimi, the scene of an impending battle between Imperial forces and troops loyal to the fallen Shogun. Kondo's wound was deep, and people marveled at the strength of body and mind which had kept him in the saddle.

A samurai holding a long sword now approached from the rear. He stopped directly behind Kondo, who held up his top-knot to facilitate the job of his executioner. The man drew his sword, sunlight flashed off polished steel, a stream of blood gushed from Kondo's neck, and the severed head dropped into the hole. Kondo Isami, the son of a peasant who had risen up to the rank of feudal lord, was dead at age thirty-five.

Presently, the head was preserved in salt, and transported some three hundred miles to Kyoto. Here it was mounted atop a bamboo stake in the soft mud along a timeless river, and left to the ravages of the elements, birds of prey and the derision of the vulgar masses.

1 *Restoration of the Reigns of Government to the Emperor*
(Courtesy of Seitoku Kinen Kaigakan)
On October 13, 1867, at the Grand Hall of Nijo Castle in Kyoto, the last
Shogun, Tokugawa Yoshinobu, announced to representatives of forty feudal
domains his decision to restore the rule of Japan to the Emperor.

2 *Negotiations for the Surrender of the Castle at Edo*
(Courtesy of Seitoku Kinen Kaigakan)
In March 1868, two days before fifty thousand Imperial troops planned to attack Edo, Katsu Kaishu, head of the Tokugawa Army, met with Saigo Kichinosuke, commander-in-chief of the Imperial forces, to negotiate the peaceful surrender of the former Shogun's castle. The historical meeting spared the city of Edo from the flames of war, and saved the lives and property of its one million inhabitants. Saigo (left) is depicted here in Japanese-style dress, but according to Katsu he was "wearing European-style clothes."

3   Sakamoto Ryoma, Tosa samurai
(Courtesy of Tokyo Ryoma-kai)
At Fukui Castletown, October 1867, just weeks before his assassination

4   Sakamoto Ryoma, Tosa samurai
(Courtesy of Kochi Prefectural Museum of History)
At Nagasaki, 1866

5 Katsu Kaishu, commissioner of the Shogun's navy
(Courtesy of Takaaki Ishiguro)
At San Francisco, 1860

6 Katsu Kaishu, commissioner of the Shogun's navy
(Courtesy of Takaaki Ishiguro)
Circa 1868 —1871

7 Takechi Hanpeita, Tosa samurai

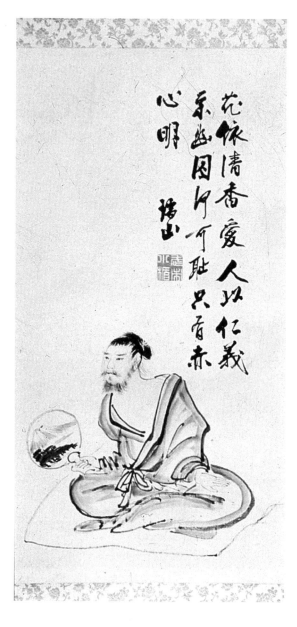

8   Takechi Hanpeita, Tosa samurai
(Courtesy of Kochi Prefectural Museum of History)
Self-portrait, drawn with brush in ink, as he languished in jail, July 1864

9 Yamanouchi Yodo, Lord of Tosa
(Courtesy of Kochi Prefectural Museum of History)

10 Saigo Kichinosuke, Satsuma samurai
(Courtesy of Kagoshima Prefectural Museum of Culture Reimeikan)

11 Tokugawa Yoshinobu, the last Shogun
(Courtesy of Takaaki Ishiguro)
Taken at Osaka Castle in March 1867, by British photographer F.W. Sutton for
The Illustrated London News. This is the only photograph of Yoshinobu of
which the photographer and date are known.

12 Kondo Isami, commander of the Shinsengumi
(Courtesy of Minato City Local History Museum)
The date and place of this photo are unknown, but believed to be February
1868, at Yokohama, about two months before his execution.

13 Yoshida Toyo, Tosa samurai and regent to Lord Yodo

14 Yamada Asaemon VIII, official executioner
(Courtesy of Yuzankaku Publishing Co.)
Taken when Asaemon VIII was fifty years old, in 1903, over twenty years after
beheading was abolished in Japan. He nevertheless posed for this photo
dressed for a beheading.

15　Shimazu Hisamitsu, Lord of Satsuma
(Courtesy of Shoko Shuseikan)

16 Bronze statue of Sakamoto Ryoma, at Katsurahama beach in Kochi
Constructed 1928

An Evil Woman

Settings

The scaffold at the execution grounds in Tokyo, January 1879

An inn in Tokyo, summer 1876

Players

Yamada Asaemon VIII (aka Yoshifusa): Official executioner in Tokyo

Takahashi Oden (aka "Evil Woman"): An attractive young woman sentenced to death for murder

An Evil Woman

The grim allure of sensational crime exceeds the bounds of history, nationality and culture. It oversteps social mores, and, on occasion, a bewitching aura of carnal desire surrounds its subject. As fate would have it, Yamada Asaemon VIII, whose given name was Yoshifusa, was so bewitched, however briefly, by an attractive young woman whom he encountered only at the scaffold. Yoshifusa was now twenty-five years old. He had been assisting his father as executioner since 1863, four years before the fall of the Tokugawa Shogunate. He had performed his first cutting test at age nine, his first beheading at twelve, and before decapitation would be abolished fourteen years after the formation of the new Meiji government, would cut off the heads of over three hundred criminals. These included celebrated political martyrs and common murderers alike, the most sensational of whom came to be known as the "Evil Woman."

Takahashi Oden was sentenced to death in a Tokyo courthouse, after a sensational trial which had lasted nearly two and a half years. On the cold, grim morning of the following day, January 30, 1879, the young woman was brought to the execution grounds behind Ichigaya Prison in the Japanese capital. The execution grounds, which the general populace aptly referred to as "hell," were situated amidst a cedar grove surrounded by one hundred yards of black fence. Within were the gallows, a recent innovation by the government in its drive to modernize and be accepted by the Western world. Death by hanging was for the perpetrators of the less serious capital offenses. In the shadow of the gallows, however, as if in defiance of occidental conventions, was the beheader's scaffold, a grim deterrent to the most heinous crimes.

Yoshifusa stood in the open courtyard some ten paces from the scaffold. A veteran at his trade, he had by now beheaded hundreds of men. As always at the execution grounds, he wore his two swords hanging from his left hip, although three years had passed since the wearing of swords had been outlawed.

Yoshifusa had read in the newspapers of the notorious Evil Woman, who, having seduced and murdered a wealthy shop-keeper for the money he had in his pocket, had been the topic of scandal in the popular press for these past two and a half years. Yoshifusa had been anxious to see her in the flesh and, when he finally did, thought that her beauty had not been exaggerated, although her cheeks were thin and pale from her long incarceration, and her eyes blindfolded. *"With skin so white as to seem transparent, and an oval face, she was a dreadful beauty,"* reported one Tokyo daily. While it might be argued that there is nothing quite so subjective as a woman's charm, be it dreadful or beatific, there was no question of the intrepidity of the Evil Woman. To be executed on this same morning was a man convicted of arson. When Oden saw the man trembling with fear, she looked him straight in the eye and, in the face of her own certain and imminent death, her voice filled with contempt, said, "What a coward you are. You call yourself a man? I'm a woman, but look at me." The combination of dreadful beauty and intrepidity aroused in Yoshifusa a disturbing carnal desire for this woman whom he now must kill.

*   *   *

Takahashi Oden was born in 1851, the illegitimate child of a high-ranking retainer of the Lord of Numata, a hereditary vassal of the Shogun. Her mother had served for a time as a domestic at her father's home. The servant was sent away before the child was born, and Oden was raised in the countryside by a farmer. There is little doubt that she grew up with the bitter pangs of an orphan, and perhaps a relentless, gnawing resentment for the father who had abandoned her. When she was fifteen, her foster father arranged her marriage. But she was unhappy with her foster father's choice, and left her home and new husband shortly after the wedding. She found employment at a local public house, but was soon dismissed for coquettish behavior with the patrons. Upon her return to the farm of her foster father, Oden was remarried, this time happily. Relieved that the girl had finally settled down to married life, the old man retired, leaving the care of his farm to the young couple. When her husband contracted leprosy three years later, Oden began a downward descent into degradation which would only end under the razor-sharp blade of the executioner's sword.

With her husband unable to work and all their money spent in treatment for the dread disease, Oden had no choice but to mortgage the farm. They eventually found themselves heavily in debt, and fled their native countryside for the harsh environs of Yokohama. In the city her husband worked as a day laborer, but was soon incapacitated by the illness which was gradually killing him. Oden found work as a maidservant by day, but to make ends meet was compelled to spend many a night at a house of ill repute. When her husband died in 1872, Oden was twenty-one years old. She became the mistress of an elderly silk dealer, who kept her in an apartment in Tokyo. Soon tiring of her benefactor, who was nearly sixty years old, Oden became reacquainted with a young wastrel whom she had known as a prostitute in Yokohama. Soon after, Oden was living in Tokyo with her new lover.

Since her lover shunned work, Oden tried to make ends meet through her good looks and knack for the lie. She borrowed money from a friend of her deceased husband in Yokohama, claiming the two faced straitened circumstances due to his continuing illness — two years after he had died. She visited the home of a friend who lived near the elderly silk dealer she had eschewed. This friend had a small child, whom Oden secretly brought to the home of the silk dealer. Claiming that the baby was his, she extorted a certain amount of money from the perplexed gentleman, before returning the child to its worried mother.

In the summer of 1876, Oden and her lover found themselves in debt. They accepted charity at a friend's home, while Oden kept her eyes open for the opportunity to escape their financial straits. Oden supposed she had discovered such an opportunity one day when she made the acquaintance of a well-to-do shop owner. By now Oden was a woman of the world, and thought she could assess easy prey when it crossed her path. She asked the shop owner to lend her a substantial sum of money which, she lied, she needed for a particular business venture. The shop owner replied that he would consider the young woman's request, but that she must first spend a night with him. On the following evening, when the two checked into an inn under the guise of man and wife, the shop owner had no inkling that concealed in Oden's handbag was a razor blade — a last resort in case her prey should not hold true to his word.

Oden was seized with rage when her premonition proved correct the next morning. Perhaps it was a deep-seated resentment for her father who had seduced her mother and abandoned his daughter which gave root to an immeasurable hate for the lascivious ways of men. But as the shop owner slept soundly, exhausted after a night of carnal pleasure at Oden's expense, she took the razor blade from her purse and, without any misgiving, calmly slit his throat. To muffle his screams, she smothered him with the bedding, as his life oozed from the gaping wound on his neck, the carotid artery and trachea completed severed.

Now she propped the head on a pillow, neatly arranged the bedding to cover the blood, and took a substantial sum of cash from the dead man's pocket. She wrote a note claiming that she had killed him to avenge the murder of her sister five years prior. She signed the note with a fake name, dressed, and, with the money packed neatly in her handbag, left the inn.

*   *   *

Oden was arrested the following evening. She now realized that the authorities would not be deceived by her fabricated tale of vengeance, and as murder was inevitably punished by death, she tenaciously tried to postpone her fate. To this end Oden was successful, for she confused and befuddled the police investigators with flagrant lies, which she invented and reinvented with a skill she had perfected since childhood. In desperation she composed a letter in her own blood, addressed to her lover, asking that he "beg someone of influence to intervene."

Help was not forthcoming, and now, on this cold, grim morning of the last day of her short, harsh life, the Evil Woman knelt at the scaffold atop a coarse straw mat. With her were four coolies, who assisted the beheader. Nearby, overseeing the entire process, stood the official Inspector of the Execution. Yoshifusa stood at Oden's left side, and although she could not see for the soft white paper cloth which covered her eyes, she seemed to stare directly into the blood vat before her. One of the coolies loosened the top of Oden's white kimono, while the others held down her shoulders, inadvertently baring the soft white skin on the nape of her neck. As Yoshifusa slowly placed his right hand on the hilt of his sword, silently reciting the four Buddhist precepts taught him by his father, to maintain composure and concentrate his mental energy, he was suddenly overcome, if only for an instant, by a pang of desire for this woman whom he must now kill. As he had never before experienced such a feeling at the scaffold, Yoshifusa was, to say the least, perplexed. He struggled to regain his composure, but the coolie behind Oden jerked both of her large toes, so that her head naturally thrust forward, exposing more of the ivory skin on her neck. As Yoshifusa brandished his sword above Oden's head, she suddenly asked to be permitted to see her lover "just one more time."

Yoshifusa's desire turned to fleeting jealousy, which was instantly subdued by a surge of hopeless pity for the woman. "Yes, I'll let you see him," he said without realizing it, as if the words had come out of their own accord.

As Yoshifusa struggled to collect himself, the woman began to scream hysterically. "I can see him? When? Now? When can I see him? Please tell me." The longer she screamed the more excited she became, and presently began shaking her shoulders wildly from side to side so that the coolies could no longer hold her down. Her kimono became undone at her knees, so that her bare legs were now visible. At his wit's end and his sword still held aloft, Yoshifusa cast a glance at the Inspector of the Execution, who shook his head. At that instant Yoshifusa brought his sword down with one swift stroke, but in the confusion struck the woman on the back of her skull. There was a loud shriek, blood gushed from the woman's head, and she deliriously repeated her final request. Her blindfold, now soaked with blood, fell from her eyes, and the four coolies again subdued the crazed woman. She recited a Buddhist prayer, "Hail Amida," twice, then fought back, momentarily freeing herself. The instant she was once again subdued, Yoshifusa brought his sword down upon the back of her neck. Oden's head fell with a soft thud into the plaster-covered blood vat, and into which the four coolies aimed the stream of blood which now surged from the headless torso.

Oden's corpse was brought to the police hospital, where over the following four days a meticulous autopsy was performed. Her most private part was carefully removed with a scalpel and preserved in alcohol as, what one historian would label, "valuable criminological data."

Tales of a
Renaissance
Samurai

Tales of a Renaissance Samurai

"I don't expect that I'll be around too long. But I'm not about to die like any average person either. I'm only prepared to die when big changes finally come, when even if I continue to live I will no longer be of any use to the country. But since I'm fairly shifty, I'm not likely to die so easily. But seriously, although I was born a mere potato digger in Tosa, a nobody, I'm destined to bring about great changes in the nation. But I'm definitely not going to get puffed up about it. Quite the contrary! I'm going to keep my nose to the ground, like a clam in the mud. So don't worry about me!"*

[Sakamoto Ryoma, in a letter to his sister, June 29, 1863, less than four and a half years before toppling the Tokugawa Shogunate, and his assassination at age thirty-two]

—— A Young Swordsman ——

On June 3, 1853, Commodore Matthew Perry of the United States Navy would lead a flotilla of warships into the bay just south of Edo, demanding a treaty between the United States and Japan. Fifteen years of bloody turmoil would ensue, during which the isolated nation would open its doors, the heretofore all-powerful Shogunate crumble, and the Son of Heaven be restored to his ancient seat of power on the Imperial throne.

In the spring of 1853, while Japan was idling away its final days of two and a half centuries of peaceful slumber, a young swordsman of the Tosa clan was leaving home for the first time. He was bound for the Shogun's distant capital of Edo, where he

---

*When Sakamoto Ryoma wrote this letter to his sister Otome in Kochi, he was working under Katsu Kaishu, to set up a naval academy in Kobe. Ryoma had fled Tosa in March of the previous year. He would die some four and a half years later, on November 15, 1867, his thirty-second birthday, just one month after indirectly convincing the last Shogun to announce his abdication and restoration of power to the Emperor.

would further his training in the way of the sword. The young swordsman was the second son of a well-to-do merchant-samurai family, in the castletown of Kochi, the center of the great domain of Tosa. Tosa was a fan-shaped mountainous province which comprised the entire southern portion of Shikoku, the smallest of the four main Japanese islands. Kochi Castletown was situated along the southern border of Tosa, just inland from the Pacific.

The young swordsman was escorted from the castletown by a train of well-wishers who bid him a safe and happy journey. The well-wishers would accompany him as far as the northwestern boarder of the domain. Summerlike weather had come to this southern land. The air was alight with the radiance of the hot Tosa sun, and the cherries were in full bloom. The escort party was in jubilant spirits until suddenly someone noticed that the young swordsman was missing. The well-wishers were alarmed, and afraid that something dreadful had happened. They immediately set out to search for him, inquiring of his whereabouts along the way. Hours passed, but still no trace of the young swordsman. One of the well-wishers, a cousin of the missing center of attention, knocked at the door of a house whose occupants were friends of the young swordsman. But there was no answer, so the cousin entered the house of his own accord. "Ryoma!" he shouted. He found the young swordsman sitting on the floor, next to his wicker traveling case, facing the wall opposite the entranceway, so that the Sakamoto family crest — a Chinese bellflower enclosed by overlapping squares to form an eight-pointed star — was plainly visible in white on the back of his black linen kimono. He was staring vacantly at a colored wood-block print hanging on the wall above him. "Ryoma," the cousin shouted again, but still no answer. Finally the cousin tapped Ryoma on the shoulder, awakening him from his trance. "Let's go," Ryoma said, and with a faint smile on his face, took up his wicker case and hurried on his way.

—— **The Young Swordsman and the Judo Master** ——

Obstinacy, while a loathsome trait in some, can be a seed of greatness in others. The obstinate refusal of a young swordsman of Tosa to accept the crippling bonds of feudal society led him to abandon his feudal clan in a dangerous and bloody quest for freedom, which would only end with the overthrow of the entire feudal system nearly six turbulent years hence, and his untimely death shortly after.

One day in Edo the young swordsman visited the *dojo* of a famous judo master. "Would you grant me the honor of a match," the young swordsman asked. The judo master consented, and without much difficulty rendered the young swordsman unconscious. Momentarily, the young swordsman regained his senses. He summoned all his courage, and stood up to confront the judo master again. This time the master threw the swordsman to the hard wooden floor with such force that he fully expected him to give up. But no sooner had the swordsman recovered a second time, than he attacked the master once again. The master now grabbed his opponent by one wrist, dragged him outside into the garden, and jammed him between two large stones, so that he should have no choice but to capitulate. Still the young swordsman would not submit. "One more time," he demanded, to which the judo master simply replied, "I guess you'll never learn." But the judo master was impressed. For the rest of his life, in fact, he never tired of telling people about "that obstinate young swordsman Sakamoto Ryoma."

—— **A Touch of the Banter** ——

High in the mountains north of Kochi Castletown, in the village of Shibamaki, surrounded by green forests and open fields and nothing else, is a big rock. The rock has a flat surface, which comprises a space nearly equal to eight tatami mats, for which reason it is known in the vernacular as "Eight Mat Rock." The rock affords a bird's-eye view of Kochi Castle, with the white plastered walls and black tiled roof of its great watchtower. Beyond the citadel lies the castletown, traversed by the Kagamigawa river, and dotted here and there with stately homes which recall a distant era. Further in the distance, beyond the mountains to the south, is the shimmering blue Pacific, spreading out to the end of the horizon of what was once a completely different world.

Just behind "Eight Mat Rock" stands the vacant former home of the Tanaka family, a relic of the days of the samurai. Encompassing the house is an old stone wall, overgrown with moss and weeds, telltale of an age gone by. During the nineteenth century these mountains were administered by the Sakamoto family, whose second son, Ryoma, would overthrow the Tokugawa Shogunate. The Tanaka family were the caretakers of the Sakamotos' land, and during his boyhood Ryoma was a frequent guest at their home. Ryosuke, the eldest son of the Tanaka family, was Ryoma's friend. The two spent a lot of time together, swimming in the pond in front of the house and hunting rabbit in the surrounding mountains.

When the author visited this rock and the former Tanaka residence, Masao Tanaka, an elderly gentleman and direct descendent of Ryosuke's several generations removed, offered the following account: "Ryoma and Ryosuke used to sit right here on this rock and drink *sake* together. They would gaze out at the Pacific, and Ryoma would talk about his wild dream of one day sailing across the ocean."

By the end of 1861 Ryoma had resolved to take the first giant step toward realizing this dream. He would flee his native Tosa, and throw off the bonds of feudalism. He would spend the six remaining years of his short, colorful life on the run for the attainment of his own personal freedom and the freedom of Japan. But first he would make a subversive journey to Choshu, as an envoy of the Tosa Loyalist Party, to exchange information with the revolutionary faction of that most revolutionary of samurai clans. When he left for Choshu one cold winter day he was badly in need of cash. "Ryoma stopped here along the way to borrow some money," Mr. Tanaka said, not without a touch of the banter. "My family lent him two gold coins. He never repaid the loan. But no matter. We still have the IOU, written by Ryosuke and signed by Sakamoto Ryoma."

—— A Man of Consequence ——

The two men were close friends. They had much in common. Both were lower-samurai of the Tosa clan, both expert swordsmen, and both leaders of the hot-blooded Tosa Loyalists who would overthrow the Shogunate and restore the Emperor to power. Takechi Hanpeita's home in Kochi was a gathering place for Men of High Purpose, who plotted and planned a coup in Tosa as a cornerstone of the greater revolution to come.

Known for their ability to consume vast amounts of *sake* at a single sitting, the young men of Tosa were wont to drink a potent local brew as a condiment to political discourse. One day, upon leaving a political meeting at Hanpeita's home, Ryoma, as was his habit, relieved himself in his friend's front garden, so that after he had left the stench of stale urine remained. When Hanpeita's wife complained about Ryoma's "sickening habit," he turned to her and sternly said, "Ryoma is a man of consequence to the nation. I think you can tolerate that much from him."

·

—— **"A Gentle Man with Sharp Insight"*** ——

By March 1862 Ryoma was disgusted with his native Tosa. He would now flee the domain, and in so doing become a ronin, a lordless samurai, an outlaw. He would join Men of High Purpose from other clans, in the revolution to restore the Emperor to power. While the crime of fleeing one's clan was among the most serious a samurai could commit, it was an integral part of the unwritten code of the warrior that once a man had determined an objective, he must be prepared to sacrifice his life in order to fulfill that objective. For Ryoma the objective was clear: building a modern navy and overthrowing the Tokugawa Bakufu.

Just now, however, the expert swordsman was without a sword. He was also without traveling money. He had made his

---

*Herein is one of two very different accounts of the circumstances behind Ryoma's flight. This account was only recently brought to the fore by Kiyoharu Omino, in his *Sakamoto Ryoma to Token* (Shinjinbutsu Oraisha, 1995). According to the other account (depicted in English in *RYOMA — Life of a Renaissance Samurai*), formerly the more widely accepted of the two, the sword which Ryoma carried when fleeing Tosa did not belong to his brother, but was given him by his second eldest sister Ei, who had received it from her estranged husband, and who was believed to have committed suicide on the night of Ryoma's flight to atone for having aided him in his crime. The validity of this account has been greatly diminished with the publication of Mr. Omino's above-mentioned book, in which he quotes the testimony some seventy years passed of an elderly woman, Mrs. Tamaki Yasuda, which the author has translated into English for this book. If Mrs. Yasuda's testimony is authentic, and circumstances certainly indicate that it is, Ryoma was seen carrying a sword wrapped in oilpaper shortly after leaving his home. As Mr. Omino points out, this was most likely a precaution taken by Ryoma so that his brother's prize sword would not be damaged by the rain. As if to bolster the validity of the Yasuda testimony, in 1988 a grave believed to be that of Ei was discovered near the Sakamoto family plot in an old Kochi cemetery. The front of the gravestone is badly weathered, so that the name of the deceased cannot be deciphered. However, the engraving on the side of the stone indicates that the grave is that of the wife of a certain Shibata Sakuemon (the name of Ei's estranged husband) and of the daughter of Sakamoto Hachihei (the name of Ei's, and Ryoma's father). While the date of death is partially worn away, it clearly falls in the Japanese chronological era which corresponds to the years between 1844 and 1847. If this is indeed Ei's grave, as the above-explained circumstances seem to indicate, she died at least fifteen years before Ryoma's flight.

criminal intentions known to his elder brother, Gombei, the patriarch of the Sakamoto family, who immediately confiscated his two swords and all of the money in his possession. Ryoma could not travel without funds, much less a sword, which he would need for protection.

As he brooded alone in his room at his brother's home in Kochi Castletown, someone opened the sliding screen door. "Otome," he said, sitting upright. Otome was Ryoma's older sister. In her hands, she carried a family heirloom — their brother's prize sword, produced by the master swordsmith Tadahiro, from the province of Hizen, which Gombei kept under lock and key, hidden somewhere in the house. "I found it," she said. "Think of it as a parting gift. Now take it and hurry, before he comes home."

"Oilpaper," Ryoma said, as he put on his jacket. "I need oilpaper."

"Oilpaper?" Otome said blankly.

"Yes. It's raining. I can't let our family heirloom get wet from the rain."

Wrapping the sword with oilpaper and carrying it over his shoulder, Ryoma left his house, prepared never to return. He hastened to the home of a relative on the outskirts of the castle-town, where he borrowed ten gold coins, and as dusk fell upon the land, walked alone through the pelting rain.

A great bronze statue of Sakamoto Ryoma was erected at the beach of Katsurahama, over sixty years after he had fled Tosa. On the day of the unveiling ceremony, in May 1928, an old woman, Mrs. Tamaki Yasuda, offered the following eyewitness account of the aftermath of Ryoma's flight.

"Ryoma's father and my father were close friends. And so, Ryoma and my older brother Eima were also very close with one another.

"Ryoma's house was quite large. He would sometimes visit our home, and we would often visit his. Ryoma and my brother used to practice fencing together at the Hineno Dojo. People say that Ryoma was large, over six feet tall, and quite a lady's man. But actually he was of average height, a dark complexion, and certainly not handsome.

"He didn't wear his hair in the style fashionable among young samurai in those days. Rather, he had a full head of hair which was constantly curled up from his hard fencing practice. He always wore a short sword in his sash in such a way that you couldn't tell at a glance if he was wearing a sword or not. He had drooping shoulders, with the left one slightly higher than the right.

"There was something about his character that differed from other young samurai of those days. He didn't swagger about or put on airs. He was a gentle man with sharp insight.

"Unlike Ryoma, his older sister Otome was large, with broad-shoulders — a truly robust woman. She was such an unusual woman! After she turned thirty she said that she couldn't be free with a man around, so she left her husband and came home. She always used to carry a pistol in her pocket. She often practiced with a halberd, and asked us if we wouldn't try it.

"I think that having such a robust woman for an older sister encouraged Ryoma in many of the things that he did.

"Two days after Ryoma had fled Tosa, his older brother Gombei came to my house. He asked my brother, 'Eima, has Ryoma been here with a sword?' Gombei placed great value on the sword that he was inquiring about. But my brother answered, 'He hasn't been here.'

"'Ryoma has not returned home since leaving on the day before yesterday,' Gombei said. 'I think he's fled Tosa. Apparently someone saw him in Susaki,* carrying over his shoulder something resembling a sword wrapped in oilpaper. But I don't know anything more than that.'

"And that's what Gombei said. I was seventeen at the time.

*Susaki was a port about eighteen miles west of Kochi Castletown.

"There was something that I remembered after Ryoma was killed in Kyoto. One day when my brother returned from the *dojo*, he said to our mother, 'Today was the first time I noticed that Ryoma has a big birthmark on his left arm. It's over seven inches around.'

"My mother knitted her brows and said, 'Poor Ryoma! That's a sign that he is in danger of dying by the sword.' After that my mother was always very worried about him. And then he was murdered. Today is the unveiling ceremony of his statue. I feel as if Ryoma has come home to Tosa after being away for over sixty years. I saw a photograph of the statue. The face, the brows, the way he wears his sword — it looks just like him."

—— The Sword Master's Daughter ——

There is a grave at an old Buddhist temple, in a mountainous region west of the sprawling megalopolis which was once the capital of the Tokugawa Shogun, in the former Province of Kai, north of Mt. Fuji, where rest the earthly remains of a sword master's daughter. Engraved on the front of the small gravestone, dated October 15, 1896, is her name, Chiba Sanako; on the back the inscription, "Sakamoto Ryoma's wife."

Ryoma practiced the way of the sword at the *dojo* of the celebrated sword master Chiba Sadakichi, one of the top fencing academies in Edo. Accepted as one of the Chiba family, he lived at his sword master's home, was initiated in his sword master's Hokushin-Itto Style at age twenty-four, and shortly after appointed to the honorable position of head of his sword master's academy. *Kenjutsu* practice at the Chiba Dojo was led by the sword master's son, Jutaro, and, upon occasion, by his eldest daughter, Sanako.

"*Sanako will be twenty-six this year,*" Ryoma wrote to his sister Otome in 1863, the year after fleeing Tosa. "*She's a good* *rider, is exceptionally skilled with a sword, knows how to use a halberd, and is physically stronger than most men. She has a slightly better face and figure than Hirai.* She was initiated (in the Hokushin-Itto Style) at age fourteen, and has a better disposition than most men. Even so, she's a quiet person who doesn't talk much."* In short, Ryoma was in love with his sword master's daughter.

"Sakamoto Ryoma asked my father for my hand in marriage," Sanako said in a magazine interview three years before her death. "But my father told us to wait until the turmoil in Japan would subside." In the meantime, the two exchanged engagement gifts. Ryoma gave Sanako a worn out kimono adorned with the Sakamoto family crest, and she imparted to him a short sword.

But Ryoma would never make good on his wedding vows. Rather, as he prophetically boasted to Otome, he was *"destined to bring about great changes in the nation"* in those most tumultuous of times. His days left in Edo were numbered. The remaining four years of his life he would spend on the move. He would eventually marry the daughter of a deceased Loyalist physician from Kyoto, whom he had rescued from dire straits, and who in turn would save his life in a near-fatal attack by Tokugawa police agents. Sanako, who remained single for the rest of her life, would go to her grave with the conviction that she was "the betrothed of Sakamoto Ryoma."

---

*Hirai Kao, the daughter of an upper-samurai of Tosa, was a former sweetheart of Ryoma's, and younger sister of Tosa Loyalist Hirai Shujiro. Shujiro was one of the three lieutenants of Takechi Hanpeita who had been forced to commit *seppuku* by the Lord of Tosa.

—— A Sword, a Gun and a Book of Law ——

On a bluff above the sandy beach at Katsurahama, just south of Kochi Castletown, stands the magnificent bronze statue of Sakamoto Ryoma. He wears his short sword at his left hip, and seems to be holding something in his right hand. But since he keeps this hand securely tucked inside his kimono, the cherished object must ever remain a mystery. Some conjecture that it is the Smith & Wesson revolver with which he protected himself in a nearly fatal ambush by Tokugawa police agents. Others venture that it is the book of international law, with which this most wanted of all political fugitives emerged victorious in a legal battle against the most powerful of all Tokugawa clans. Regardless, the spirit of this most remarkable of samurai certainly looms on high, as his earthbound image, eyes strained in a perpetual squint, gazes out at eternity and the vast Pacific.

One day the outlaw Sakamoto Ryoma encountered a friend in the streets of Kyoto. The man wore a long sword at his side, as was popular during those bloody days. Ryoma took one look at the sword, and said, "That sword's too long. If you get caught in close quarters you won't be able to draw the blade." Showing the man his own sword, Ryoma said, "This is a better length."

Soon after, the man replaced his long sword with a shorter one, and showed it to Ryoma. Laughing derisively, Ryoma produced a pistol from his breast pocket. He fired a shot in the air, and with a wide grin on his face said, "This is the weapon I've been using lately." The two friends met again some time later, when Ryoma took from his pocket a book of international law. "In the future," he said, "we are going to have to learn more than just the arts of war. I've been reading this recently, and it is so very interesting."

—— **The Fugitive and His Plans** ——

The political fugitive was forever guided by an uncanny fore-sight, so that once he got it into his mind to do something he could not rest until the job was done. He was driven by an inner force to act, to strive, and to risk his life for goals which others could not readily comprehend. His behavior seemed preposter-ous to his family, an enigma to his comrades in the revolution. A leader in the movement to overthrow the Shogunate, he even-tually sided with one of the enemy to achieve this goal. A former xenophobe who once promised his father to "cut off a few for-eign heads," he now advocated free international trade to strengthen the nation. Outlandish by nature? Perhaps! But in his outlandishness lay the key to his greatness and the source of his deepest sorrow.

Having brokered the all-important military alliance between the Satsuma and Choshu clans, having established Japan's first modern trading company to run guns for the revolutionary forces, and having devised a plan whereby the Shogun had in the previous month peacefully relinquished the reins of power to the Emperor, this political fugitive who had never held an official post now wrote the blueprint for the new Japanese gov-ernment, and drew up a list of men to fill the most important posts. Placing both documents into his pocket, the fugitive, accompanied by an assistant, proceeded to the Satsuma estate in Kyoto to see Saigo Kichinosuke, the most powerful man in Japan.

Soon Ryoma and his assistant sat with Saigo and two other men in a drawing room at the Satsuma estate. Saigo read both documents, then gave the fugitive a puzzled look. "Sakamoto-san," he said, almost suspiciously, "your name is not on this list." Saigo's suspicion was not uncalled-for, although he had never before doubted Ryoma's integrity. But for the man who had devised the plan for the Shogun to relinquish power not to include himself in the new government was beyond Saigo's comprehension.

Ryoma nodded slowly. "You ought to know that I could never stand a government job," he said.

"What do you mean?" Saigo asked, drawing a grimace from Ryoma, who continued. "Leaving for work every morning at the same time, and coming home every evening at the same time would make me crazy with boredom."

Ryoma's thinking was not quite as outlandish as it may have seemed. To be sure, he had spent the past five and a half years struggling and risking his life to topple the Tokugawa Shogunate, and to achieve a strong, democratic government in Japan. But this had never been his ultimate goal, which was rather the attainment of simple freedom. Now that he had finally eliminated the biggest obstacle to this goal, which was the Shogunate, Ryoma wanted more than anything else the freedom to be, the freedom to think and the freedom to act as he chose. But Ryoma's was by no means a selfish goal; rather his own personal freedom was deeply intertwined with that of his friends', and with the well-being of the new nation, which depended more than anything else on economic development through international trade. And it was on the well-being of Japan which Ryoma had based all his hopes and dreams.

"If you're not going to be in the new government," Saigo asked, "what do you plan to do?"

Ryoma leaned back against a wooden post, folded his arms at his chest and said with his usual nonchalance, "I think that I just might give the whole world to my trading company." The three Satsuma men were puzzled by Ryoma's curious remark, as was Ryoma's assistant, Mutsu Yonosuke, who would become one of Japan's greatest foreign ministers. Although Yonosuke would never know exactly what Ryoma meant by the remark, he would never forget it. From this day on, and for years to come, he was wont to compare the political outlaw who was his mentor with the most influential man of the most powerful domain in Japan: "It was at that time," he would repeat over and over again, "that I realized Ryoma was a far greater man than even Saigo himself." Saigo agreed, one day offering this evaluation of his outlandish friend: "There are famous men in this world, and I have associated with many of them. But I have never met anyone with the immeasurable magnanimity that was Ryoma's."

Anecdotes, Yarns and Other Vignettes

Anecdotes, Yarns and Other Vignettes

—— **An Unruly Man** ——

*By March 1863 opposition to the foreign treaties had so inten-
sified that the Shogun himself was compelled to travel to Kyoto
to promise the Emperor to expel the foreigners by the tenth of
the following May. This first visit to Kyoto by a Shogun in over
two centuries displayed Edo's diminishing ability to dominate
Japan, emboldening anti-Tokugawa Loyalists throughout the
nation.*

A hard rain fell against the pageantry of high ceremony in the
Imperial capital. The Shogun on horseback in full military
dress, followed by a retinue of his most elite retainers and the
most powerful feudal lords in Japan, escorted the Emperor,
seated in his palanquin amidst an Imperial procession. The procession moved steadily through the town, toward the Imperial
Kamo Shrine in the center of the city. Throngs lined the way for
a once-in-a-lifetime chance to catch a glimpse of the person of
the Tokugawa Shogun.

Among the throngs, near the Sanjo Bridge, stood Takasugi
Shinsaku, a radical leader of Choshu, the most outwardly anti-
Tokugawa and xenophobic of the samurai clans. Takasugi was
notorious for his unruliness, and now, amidst the pouring rain
and most of the populace of the Imperial capital, he suddenly
screamed the Shogun's ancient and official title, "Commander
in Chief of the Expeditionary Forces Against the Barbarians."
The title had not been uttered in public during the two and half
centuries of Tokugawa rule, until Takasugi now challenged the
Shogun, in a voice filled with irony and wrath, to hold good his
xenophobic promise. Had the outrage been committed elsewhere than in the Imperial capital, the Shogun's bodyguards
would have cut down the blasphemer on the spot. But Kyoto had
of late become the gathering place of anti-Tokugawa samurai,
and the Shogun no longer commanded his unchallenged author-

ity of the past.

—— **One Stormy Summer Day** ——

Takechi Hanpeita was revered among Men of High Purpose throughout Japan as a master swordsman, accomplished painter, brilliant Confucian scholar, stoic warrior and samurai par excellence. As leader of the revolutionary Tosa Loyalist Party, he commanded recognition and respect at the Imperial Court in Kyoto; and as mastermind of political assassination, he terrorized the streets of the ancient Imperial capital, challenged the authority of the powerful Lord of Tosa, and the rule of the Tokugawa Shogun.

Hanpeita was at home with his wife Tomi, one stormy summer day. The air inside the house was heavy with humidity, but Tomi had closed the wooden shutter doors to keep the rain out. So violently did the torrent fall upon the thatched roof, that she had hung a small wooden bucket from a horizontal beam in the doorway to catch the leaking rainwater. After the storm subsided, she asked her husband to take down the bucket, nearly filled to the brim. Hanpeita stood up from his desk, where he had been peering over a volume of ancient Chinese literature, and without speaking, removed the bucket from the beam. Suddenly the heavy bucket slipped from his hands, completely drenching him. Still silent and showing no emotion on his sullen, pale face, Hanpeita simply removed his light cotton kimono, but not his wet loincloth. Wiping his face with a clean towel his wife now handed him, he calmly returned to his desk, still wearing the loincloth. The stoic warrior would not be seen naked by anyone, including his wife.

—— **A Philosopher of the People** ——

That Count Katsu's humble birth influenced his actions throughout his life is beyond question. That as an elite shogunal official he was in league with revolutionaries, political outlaws, and other enemies of state is a known fact. Following are five verbal accounts* by the former commissioner of the Tokugawa Navy and most powerful man in Edo — and more lately minister of the Japanese Navy and councilor of state. These accounts manifest Katsu Kaishu's constant sympathy and occasional preference for outcasts in a strict hierarchical society which disparaged the lower classes and severely punished nonconformity even after the collapse of the feudal system.

"Politics do not work on theory alone. A person must closely scrutinize the realities of life and men, and be well informed of the state of things. It is much better to speak with an uneducated illiterate than to listen to lame political discussion. An illiterate is genuine and pure, and what's more will always be reasonable about life.

"When the Imperial forces were advancing upon Edo Castle I did a lot of thinking, and rallied together a group of so-called rogues. I had a really hard time of it. After leaving the government office each day I would catch a palanquin to visit the leaders of these rogues. And although I did have a hard time of it, it was actually quite amusing.

"I said to them, 'I'd like to confide in you by asking a favor. And since you don't care about the power of money or the authority of the Shogun, I've come here to see you.'

"'We see,' they said. 'If we can be of service, feel free to call upon us any time.' I really admired their openheartedness.

"The reason that there were relatively few incidents of arson and burglary during the anarchy which followed the Imperial

---

*Given during the two-year period of 1897 and 1898. Katsu Kaishu died in January 1899, ten days before the seventy-sixth anniversary of his birth.

forces' arrival at Edo, was because I had arranged for the assistance of the so-called rouges."

*

Count Katsu was not one to turn his nose up to anyone.

"One time somebody must have seen me going into a brothel called the Hell House. When Prince Sanjo* admonished me about it, I simply said, 'The owner's an old friend of mine.' Prince Sanjo was quite surprised, and told me that, in any case, it just wasn't proper for a councilor of state to frequent a place like that. But I didn't understand what all the fuss was about. The place might have been a brothel, but in my eyes it was just a place that belonged to an old friend of mine."

*

Then there were the three criminals who earned the great man's amazed admiration and his acquittal of their crimes soon after the fall of the Shogunate.

"One of them committed robberies while in the employ of a stable keeper in Edo. Having stolen a large amount of money, he hid it somewhere and left the city, then returned about a year later to live off the booty. When this money ran out, he stole some more, hiding it as before. Next he went to the Kyoto region, and again lived off the money he had hidden.

"But he did everything so well! Outwardly he pretended not to have any money at all, working diligently as a stable keeper's helper. I was truly impressed by the combination of his daring and prudence. But what really amazed me was that he had broken out of jail in broad daylight, dressed in blue prisoner's garb."

---

*Sanjo Sanetomi (1838 - 1891) was a radical leader of court nobles instrumental in the restoration of the Emperor to power. After the restoration he became an important leader of the Meiji government, serving as chief advisor and spokesman of the Emperor.

"The second one was also a thief. While most people would turn pale under police interrogation, this man answered all the questions very calmly. Then just when everyone thought he had been falsely charged, and after he had made his final plea, he removed his jacket, and sitting arrogantly with his legs crossed, said,* 'Go ahead, tie me up. There's no reason for me to escape now. Maybe it was my fate to be arrested. I'll now confess to everything.' And that's just what he did, calmly admitting his guilt.

"Then after the Restoration I let everyone go, thinking that killing fifty or sixty prisoners wouldn't rid the world of burglars anyway. Most of the prisoners cried tears of joy, thanking me for sparing their lives. Not this man. When I told him he was free, all he said was 'Oh, really?' without ever changing the expression on his face."

"The other prisoner was a woman around thirty years old. I wanted to hear the details of her crimes, so I had everyone leave the room, and, sitting face-to-face with her, started the interrogation. She began her confession by saying that she had never told anyone before, and that she would tell only me.

"'There were so many womanizers who used to approach me, attracted by my good looks, I suppose. One day I pretended to be attracted to one who had lots of money. Well, after we started doing it, I grabbed his you-know-what and wrung it so hard that I killed him. I took his money, got out of there and had nothing more to do with the matter. When the doctor examined the body, there were no wounds. They had no way of knowing what happened. I've killed five men in all.'

"Now, isn't that the most daring thing you've ever heard?" Katsu said sardonically, then in a more somber tone summed up

---

*In a formal situation such as a police interrogation, protocol required a person to sit properly — legs and feet tucked underneath, back straight, hands resting atop the thighs.

his brief commentary on the human condition. "All of them were the way they were by nature. Had they received a proper education, they would certainly have been a force to be reckoned with. But regrettably each of them were born to such humble circumstances that they never had a chance to make something of themselves.

"However, maybe the world is a better place because they never had an opportunity to do any real damage, under the lame pretext of serving the nation or for some other political motive. At any rate, I could never hold a candle to any of them."

—— **A Horror Beyond Words** ——

In September 1863, the Lord of Tosa unleashed a crackdown against renegade samurai of his own clan. Takechi Hanpeita and his followers in the outlawed Tosa Loyalist Party were arrested in Kochi Castletown and jailed. Loyalists in the outlying areas of Tosa who had evaded arrest were outraged. Under the slogan "Do not kill Takechi-sensei," these men petitioned the release of their comrades. In the following September, twenty-three of them were rounded up by the authorities, and two days later brought to a place along a river. The following is an eye-witness account of a "horror beyond words," as told by the wife of a comrade of the twenty-three.

When they were going to behead the twenty-three men along the Naharigawa river, they came and asked my husband to serve as witness to the execution. He was sick at the time, and unable to oblige. I went in his stead. When I arrived at the riverside, I saw the twenty-three seated on straw mats all in a row. In front of them had been dug a trench about six feet wide and six feet deep. They proceeded to behead each man, one after the next. When a head had been severed, the body tried to stand up. But the executioners kicked the bodies from behind, so that they fell forward into the trench. I was not allowed to leave until all twenty-three had been beheaded. It was a horror beyond words, so that now I wipe the tears from my eyes in recollection.

—— **A Notorious Toady** ——

It is said that more men of the Shinsengumi were killed for violating the corps' draconian code than died in battle. The number of victims of the code is unknown. Of the twenty-two of the corps' most noted officers, six were assassinated by their own men, three were ordered to commit seppuku for violating the code, two were executed, and only three survived the revolution. One of the survivors erected a stone monument for the repose of the souls of his dead comrades. Engraved in this monument are the names of sixty-five men, many victims of the code, among them a notorious toady.

Shinsengumi Number Five Squad Leader Takeda Kanryusai was a notorious toady. He was constantly flattering the corps leaders Kondo Isami and Hijikata Toshizo. He had been recruited into the corps not for his ability with a sword, but for his extensive knowledge of an old and tried Japanese school of military tactics. Takeda was put in charge of drilling the entire corps, a position which, along with his reputation for toadyism, earned him the ire of scores of swordsmen who were made of a far tougher substance than he. Takeda savored the glory of his position, and when he wasn't flattering his superiors, tended to boast to his peers of his abilities and achievements.

When the Bakufu began Westernizing its military under the tutelage of the French, the Shinsengumi received modern rifles and orders to drill in the European style. Not only was Takeda disliked by his peers, but he now found that he no longer wielded the respect of the corps' leaders. Feeling slighted, he began to secretly frequent the estate of the Satsuma clan, in the town of Fushimi just south of Kyoto. When it was called to the attention of Kondo and Hijikata that Takeda was divulging confidential information to Satsuma, the two leaders took immediate action.

One evening in September 1866, Commander Kondo held a small "farewell party" for Takeda, to which the officers of the corps, including Takeda, were summoned.

With the group assembled in the appointed banquet room, and *sake* served, Kondo looked at Takeda and said with a forced smile, "I have heard that you will be leaving the corps to serve Satsuma." Kondo did not need mention that according to the code of the Shinsengumi quitting the corps for any reason was punishable by death.

"I have only been considering the idea of joining the Satsuma men to gather information," Takeda lied, his voice cracking from fear. "But I haven't made any final decisions yet."

"A spy," Kondo roared, clapping his hands. "A great plan. You should go to the Satsuma estate tonight."

"But..."

"Shinohara and Saito," Kondo called the names of two of the officers. "I want you to escort him to the Satsuma estate in Fushimi."

Takeda shuddered inside. While he was on friendly terms with Shinohara, he had never gotten along well with Saito. Furthermore, the latter man, who had been drinking this evening, had a reputation as a bad drunk and a propensity to draw his sword after just a few drinks. Takeda tried to refuse Kondo's offer, insisting he would travel alone.

"We'll have nothing of the kind," Kondo said, his voice filled with irony. "You will be safer with an escort."

As if resigned to his fate, Takeda soon departed with the two others. They traveled in single file along the narrow highway toward Fushimi — Takeda in the lead, followed closely by Saito, with Shinohara in the rear. Shortly after eight o'clock the party approached a bridge, desolate in the darkness. Whether Takeda sensed that death was upon him, or that Shinohara's presence afforded him peace of mind during his final moments will never be known. But the instant that Saito drew his long sword, a metallic chaffing sound of polished steel certainly filled Takeda's brain, and before he could draw his own blade, his entire backside was sliced open from right shoulder to left hip.

Saito kneeled over the bloody corpse, and removed both swords. "For all his boasting to the contrary," he said to Shinohara, "Takeda was an easy kill." Saito stood up and brushed the dust from the scabbards of the slain man's swords. "Let's go," he said, and without looking back, the two men retraced their footsteps in the darkness.

—— **Drastic Measures** ——

The samurai of Satsuma were renowned for their courage, fierceness in battle and unyielding resolve to die. A school of fencing prevalent in Satsuma advocated that a swordsman must never depend solely on his sword. If a man should somehow lose his sword, he must "shatter the enemy's head with his fist." One celebrated sword master of this clan stressed that the enemy must be killed with the first strike. "If the enemy should parry your first attack," he professed, "you must hurl yourself at him and die." In the notorious battle at the Teradaya inn in Fushimi, one Satsuma man's sword was severed at the hilt. Perceiving inevitable death, he threw his broken weapon to the floor and charged his opponent, pinning him against the wall. "Drive your sword through us," he told a comrade, who immediately drew his blade, impaling both men.* Among the most lethal of Satsuma swordsmen was one Nakamura Hanjiro, sometimes known as "The Butcher," of whom it was said could "draw and resheath his blade three times before a drop of rainwater falling from the eaves could reach the ground."

By September 1867, just one month before the abdication of the last Shogun, Nakamura Hanjiro, a devoted follower of Saigo Kichinosuke, had for some time suspected that the celebrated military scientist Akamatsu Kosaburo could not be trusted. The Satsuma men, led by Saigo, were secretly planning to crush of the Tokugawa with military force. Akamatsu was a leading advocate of uniting the Tokugawa with the Imperial Court, which put him at odds with the Satsuma men. Nevertheless, Akamatsu, a samurai of the Ueda clan, had been serving at the Satsuma estate in Kyoto as guest artillery instructor. The Lord of Ueda was a hereditary vassal of the Tokugawa. When Akamatsu suddenly received orders to return to his native clan, Nakamura worried that the scholar might leak vital information about Satsuma's war plans. Investigation into the scholar's doings suggested that he was a Tokugawa spy. It was now that "The Butcher," either of his own accord or at the bidding of his superiors, resolved to take drastic measures.

One afternoon, while walking with another Satsuma samurai in the southwestern part of Kyoto, Nakamura encountered Akamatsu heading toward them. Although Akamatsu carried a pistol, he did not suspect the intentions of the Satsuma men. He had always been treated with the utmost respect at their Kyoto estate, and Nakamura himself was one of his students. Just as Akamatsu was about to pass them, Nakamura drew his long sword. The scholar pulled his pistol from his breast pocket, but to no avail. Before he could fire, his upper torso was sliced wide open from left shoulder to right side, and as he fell, the second Satsuma man delivered another blow from behind. The assassins had intended to take the head, but for fear of being discovered in the light of day, retreated without the trophy.

*For a detailed account of this battle, see *RYOMA — Life of a Renaissance Samurai.*

A Brief Historical Background of the Meiji Restoration

 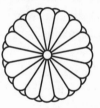

A Brief Historical Background of the Meiji Restoration

On June 3, 1853,* Commodore Matthew Perry of the United States Navy led a flotilla of warships into Sagami Bay, to the Port of Uraga, just south of the Japanese capital. The Americans found a technologically backward, though intricately complicated, island nation, under the rule of the House of Tokugawa, that had been almost completely isolated from the rest of the world for two and a half centuries.** Whether or not the Americans realized the far-reaching effect of their visit, they now set into motion a *coup de theatre* which fifteen years hence would transform the conglomerate of feudal domains into a single, unified country. When the fifteenth and last Shogun abdicated his rule and restored the Emperor to his ancient seat of power in 1868, Japan was well on its way to becoming an industrialized nation, rapidly modernizing and westernizing in a unique Japanese sense.

Under Tokugawa rule, Japan consisted of some 260 fiefdoms overseen by samurai, and ruled by a feudal lord, or *daimyo*. The Shogun, Head of the House of Tokugawa, was the mightiest *daimyo* of all. He dominated the Japanese nation from his military government at Edo, which was known throughout the land as the Tokugawa Bakufu. All feudal lords were required by the Law of Alternate Attendance to maintain official estates in Edo, where they were obligated to reside in alternate years. During their absence from the Shogun's capital, the lords were required to leave their wives and heirs at their Edo residences as virtual hostages, a protective measure of the Bakufu against insurrection in the provinces.

Perry's sudden demand for a treaty sparked the greatest

*July 8, 1853, in the Gregorian calendar.

**All foreign affairs, including trade, were restricted to the port city of Nagasaki, in western Kyushu, where Japan had dealt exclusively with the Dutch and, to a lesser extent, the Chinese and Koreans since 1639.

uproar in the theretofore peaceful history of the Tokugawa Bakufu. There had been several incidents in the past of foreign ships appearing off the Japanese coast, but this was the first time that a flotilla of heavily armed warships — "Black Ships," as the Japanese called them — had threatened Edo. The Japanese had never seen such magnificent ships. Two were steamers which could move about freely, independent of sails or the winds. All four were mounted with great guns on each side, totaling eighty in all, with enough firepower to devastate the wooden city.

Until now, the Shogunate had been more concerned with preserving its rule than competing technologically with foreign countries. As long as the government could keep the foreigners out, the rest of the nation would have to abide by its dictates. To prevent would-be insurgents from secretly traveling overseas, the Bakufu had for centuries banned the building of large ships. As a result, Japan had become so technologically backward that it was now unable to defend itself from the Western powers that threatened to dominate Asia.

The Americans presented the Bakufu with a critical dilemma. The military government feared that acquiescence might lead to subjugation, but rejection trigger a war it could not hope to win. The Japanese had received reports of the Opium War during the previous decade, through which Great Britain dominated China. The Bakufu gradually adopted an official policy of *Opening the Country*, while samurai throughout Japan violently advocated *Expelling the Barbarians*.

Coerced by Perry's gunboat diplomacy to sign a treaty with the United States in March 1854, the Bakufu completed similar treaties with Great Britain, France, Russia and The Netherlands shortly after. While these initial treaties did not provide for foreign trade, they entitled foreign ships to purchase food and other necessities from the Japanese, and assured them amicable treatment in case of shipwreck off the Japanese coast. Two ports were opened; one at the village of Shimoda, just southwest of

Edo; the other at Hakodate, on the distant northern island of Ezo. Samurai throughout Japan resented the intrusion of the barbarians, and scorned the Bakufu's weakness *vis-à-vis* the foreigners.

In the summer of 1856, the American envoy Townsend Harris set up a United States Consulate at a Buddhist temple in Shimoda to negotiate Japan's first commercial treaty. Protocol demanded that before the Bakufu signed such a treaty it must receive permission from the Imperial Court in Kyoto. Although the Emperor had not ruled in over a thousand years, his prestige of ancient times remained. The first Tokugawa Shogun had only obtained his rank after being conferred by the Emperor with the official title of "Commander in Chief of the Expeditionary Forces Against the Barbarians." But then-Emperor Komei (reign 1846 - 1867) was a chronic xenophobe, and the Imperial Court naturally opposed contacts with foreigners. As the commercial treaty with the United States materialized, samurai throughout Japan began to embrace xenophobic, and consequently anti-Bakufu and pro-Imperial, sentiment.

With the foreign issue weighing heavily upon its shoulders, the Tokugawa also faced the critical problem of shogunal succession. While the Bakufu desperately needed a strong leader in these pressing times, Shogun Tokugawa Iesada was mentally retarded, and childless at age thirty-five. Within the Bakufu arose two opposing positions concerning succession. On one side were the 145 hereditary lords, direct retainers of the Tokugawa, whose ancestors had supported the first Shogun during the great wars at the turn of the seventeenth century. These lords, who occupied all the important governmental posts, were most concerned with preserving the status quo. They argued that shogunal succession must be decided according to tradition, and thus be given to the child-Lord of Kii, a close relative of the Shogun. Opposing the hereditary lords was a small group of practical *daimyo* who argued that succession should be given to the more able Lord Yoshinobu, the son of the Lord of Mito. While both Kii and Mito were among the elite Three Tokugawa Branch Houses which descended from the three youngest sons of the first Shogun, tradition favored the Lord of Kii.

The Lord of Mito was a staunch exclusionist who advocated *Expelling the Barbarians*. He argued that his Kii cousin, at age twelve, was simply too young to rule. Opposing Mito was a powerful man by the name of Ii Naosuke, Lord of Hikone, the largest of the hereditary clans. Lord Ii advocated trade with the West as a means to fortify the nation, financially and techno-logically. Japan was now divided into two factions, which rallied around the powerful feudal lords of Mito and Hikone, respectively. The Mito faction claimed that the Shogun was merely an Imperial agent, who at the beginning of the seventeenth century had been commissioned by the Emperor to protect Japan from foreign invasion. These Imperial Loyalists insisted that true political authority rested with the Emperor. They pointed out that since its establishment the Bakufu had justified its rule by claiming to ease and protect the Son of Heaven, handling all governmental affairs for him. They blamed the Shogun for dishonoring and upsetting His Sacred Majesty, through failure to deal firmly with the foreigners. They argued that since the Shogun was no longer able to keep the foreigners out, the Emperor and his court must be restored to power to save the nation. As a result, the national government gradually developed into a twofold structure: while the Bakufu continued to rule at Edo, the ancient Imperial Court was undergoing a political renaissance at Kyoto. With this came the political education of young court nobles in Kyoto, who throughout the reign of the Tokugawa had been completely excluded from government. Even the Emperor himself was a political novice. He harbored no anti-Bakufu designs, and his chronic xenophobia was due to a fear of things Western brought on by ignorance of the outside world.

When the Bakufu petitioned the Imperial Court to sanction

a commercial treaty, they were flatly refused. The court at Kyoto instructed Edo to abide by existing Tokugawa institutions. It argued that violation of the laws handed down by the first Shogun would disturb the people and make it impossible to preserve lasting tranquillity.

In 1858, however, the Bakufu appointed Lord Ii as regent, investing him with dictatorial power. Regent Ii arranged for the child-Lord of Kii to succeed the imbecilic Shogun, who died soon after. The young *daimyo* of Kii now became the fourteenth Shogun, Tokugawa Iemochi, under whom Regent Ii realized a commercial treaty with the United States without Imperial sanction. The regent's action was considered nothing short of *lese majesty* by the proponents of *Imperial Reverence and Expelling the Barbarians*, a new battle cry among radical samurai. To subdue his enemies, the dictator unleashed his Great Purge, which began with the arrest of over one hundred advocates of *Imperial Reverence and Expelling the Barbarians*, including court nobles, Bakufu officials, feudal lords and samurai. Unprecedented in scope and severity, the punishment was harshest on the Lord of Mito and his retainers. The Lord of Mito was placed under house arrest; his son, who had recently succeeded him as *daimyo*, was confined to his residence and prohibited from performing his official duties; another son, Lord Yoshinobu, who would eventually become the last Shogun, was forced to retire from political life and placed under house confinement.

On the unseasonably snowy morning of March 3, 1860, Regent Ii was assassinated by eighteen swordsmen of the Mito and Satsuma clans. The attack came as the regent's palanquin was escorted by an entourage of bodyguards through Sakurada Gate, a main entrance to Edo Castle. The incident put an abrupt end to the dictator's reign of terror, and unleashed a wave of assassinations which would not cease until after the downfall of the Bakufu seven years later.

In a vain attempt to stem the tide of revolution, the Bakufu now proposed a union between Edo and Kyoto, to be secured by a marriage between Shogun Iemochi and Princess Kazu, a younger sister of Emperor Komei. Through a *Union of Court and Camp*, the Bakufu hoped to regain absolute authority, which had diminished with the coming of Perry, and more recently with the assassination of the regent. The government reasoned that once the Princess was married to the Shogun and living within the confines of Edo Castle, a Loyalist attack on the Bakufu would be nothing short of an assault on the Imperial Family. The radicals would no longer be able to use their claim of "loyal dedication to the Son of Heaven" as an excuse to act against the Shogun, who would be directly related to the Emperor. In order to persuade Emperor Komei to sanction the marriage proposal, the Bakufu claimed that such a bond would unite the hearts of the Japanese people, and consolidate the nation to expel the foreigners. In July 1860, the Bakufu pledged the impossible: to expel the foreigners from Japan if the Princess would marry the Shogun, an offer which the chronically xenophobic Emperor could ill refuse.

At the vanguard of the revolution stood the great domains of Satsuma, Choshu and Tosa. Their *daimyo* were among the most powerful "outside lords," whose ancestors, in contrast to those of the hereditary lords, had become retainers of the first Tokugawa Shogun only after he had defeated his enemies during the great wars at the outset of the seventeenth century. The founder of the Tokugawa dynasty had confiscated vast portions of the Satsuma and Choshu domains to ensure that his vanquished enemies could never pose a threat to his family's rule. However, unlike the Lord of Choshu, who was overtly anti-Bakufu, the crafty Satsuma *daimyo* was weary of Tokugawa clout. Satsuma and Choshu were traditional enemies, and the long and festering hatred between the two threatened the revolutionary movement. Further complicating the political landscape was the relationship between the influential Lord of Tosa and the Bakufu. Unlike Satsuma and Choshu, whose ancestors had been chastised for having fought against the first Shogun, the Lord of Tosa had been rewarded with his vast domain for not having opposed the Tokugawa. He would never side against the Bakufu, who were his ancestral beneficiaries fifteen generations past. Within Tosa, however, had developed a staunchly pro-Imperialist movement among the lower-samurai of that clan. The Tosa Loyalists, with the radical samurai of Satsuma and Choshu, now replaced their battle cry of *Imperial Reverence and Expelling the Barbarians*, with the more revolutionary *Toppling the Bakufu and Imperial Loyalism.*

The wedding between the Shogun and the princess took place in December 1861, exacerbating anti-Tokugawa and xenophobic sentiment throughout Japan. By the summer of 1862, hordes of *ronin* — renegade samurai who had fled their clans to fight for the Loyalist cause — had gathered in Kyoto. The formerly tranquil Imperial capital was now transformed into a sea of blood. Loyalists crying *"Heaven's Revenge"* drew their lethal swords on the enemies of their cause, as murder of Tokugawa supporters became a daily occurrence.

With the Shogun having set May 10, 1863, as the date by which he would expel the foreigners, Choshu made its plans accordingly. Aware that Edo had no intention of using military force to carry out its promise, the Choshu rebels had a dual-purpose in mind when they gathered at Shimonoseki Strait at the southwestern point of Choshu: improving their status among the xenophobic court at the expense of Satsuma, and further diminishing Bakufu prestige by attacking foreign ships passing through the strait.

Shimonoseki Strait, which separated the southern island of Kyushu from the Honshu mainland, was a point of crossing for foreign ships traveling between Yokohama and Nagasaki. On the morning of May eleventh, an American merchant ship bound for Nagasaki was suddenly chased and fired upon by two Choshu warships as it passed through the strait. On the twenty-third of the same month a French dispatch-boat crossing these waters was similarly attacked, as was a Dutch corvette three days later.

Retaliation was swift. At dawn on June first, the American sloop of war *Wyoming* entered Shimonoseki Strait. Choshu immediately fired their outdated bronze cannon from three separate batteries along the coast. The *Wyoming*, however, unlike the three foreign ships recently attacked in these waters, was aware of the inferior firing range of the Choshu guns. Keeping a safe distance from the Choshu batteries, the Americans fired relentlessly, and within minutes had sunk two Choshu warships and badly damaged a third. Just an hour after the first shot had been fired, the *Wyoming* left the startled Choshu domain for Yokohama. The French retaliated on the morning of June fifth, pounding the Shimonoseki coast with two heavily armed warships. After destroying a Choshu battery, three hundred French troops landed on Shimonoseki, burning to the ground a surrounding village and, to the horror of the xenophobic Choshu samurai, temporarily occupying the remaining batteries. At dusk of the same day the French gathered up their dead and injured, reboarded their ships and departed the humiliated Choshu domain for Yokohama.

Until now, the Loyalists had been confident that if it came to combat on land the foreigners would be no match for the fighting spirit of the samurai. The French proved them wrong, and the leadership of Choshu had once and for all realized that repelling the barbarians by force was impossible.

Satsuma learned a similar lesson in the following July, when Kagoshima, the capital of that domain, was bombarded and badly destroyed by British warships. (A detailed account of the reasons and circumstances of this bombardment are provided in the sketch titled *To Cut a Foreigner*.)

Despite their humiliation at the hands of the foreigners, the anti-Bakufu Loyalists in Kyoto, led by Choshu, flourished in the summer of 1863. It seemed that they had gained the complete backing of the Imperial Court, while those in favor of a *Union of Court and Camp* were at their wits' ends trying to suppress them. Then, at the bidding of Edo, Satsuma secretly set out to destroy Choshu.

In mid-August, the Aizu clan, a staunch Tokugawa ally, and Satsuma formed a military alliance, giving Satsuma and Tokugawa sympathizers at court influence over Imperial decree at the exclusion of Choshu. The stage was now set for a *coup d'etat* in Kyoto, and a dramatic reversal of Loyalist fortunes. On August eighteenth, under the cover of night, the Lord of Aizu entered the Imperial Palace, while heavily armed Satsuma and Aizu troops seized the Nine Forbidden Gates. Soon after, five feudal lords under Imperial decree led their own troops to fortify the Imperial guard of Aizu and Satsuma, barring entrance to the palace by enemies of the Tokugawa.

The Choshu troops responded by storming one of the Nine Forbidden Gates, but to no avail. Like the eight other entrances to the palace, it too had been seized by their heavily armed Satsuma and Aizu foes. Betrayed, the Choshu men aimed their cannon at the gate, but when they received a written order from the Emperor to immediately retreat, this most dedicated of all Loyalist clans had to obey, or else be branded an "Imperial Enemy."

The defeated Choshu Loyalists returned home to plan a countercoup. Into exile with them went the idol of anti-foreign *Imperial Loyalism*, Lord Sanjo Sanetomi, and six other radical court nobles. The political stage in Kyoto had taken a complete turnabout in a single night, as the pro-Bakufu faction at court regained power.

The countercoup came the following July. Two thousand Choshu troops consisting of four divisions sailed into Osaka Bay, and set up camps at four points surrounding Kyoto, with an additional two thousand en route from Choshu. The Loyalists would march into the Imperial capital to appeal to the court the innocence of the Seven Banished Nobles, and the Lord of Choshu, who was now an "Imperial Enemy." They would inform the court of their intention to remain in Kyoto "to investigate the activities of the ruffians," namely Satsuma and Aizu. If their entreaties were not accepted, they would attack the troops guarding the Imperial Palace, retake the court, and reinstate the Seven Banished Nobles.

The Bakufu forces, however, outnumbered the Choshu Army tenfold. In the face of some fifty thousand pro-Tokugawa troops on high alert in Kyoto, the rebels refused to retreat. Instead they prepared their weapons and watched for an opportunity to strike. Meanwhile, several Imperial representatives who were secretly sympathetic to Choshu's demands to expel the foreigners urged the court to recognize Choshu. Other nobles, backing Aizu-Satsuma, insisted that yielding to Choshu's demands would only harm Tokugawa prestige, and so weaken the nation. "Resist Choshu now or it will be uncontrollable later," they warned. Lord Yoshinobu of Mito, recently appointed as the Tokugawa's Inspector General of the Forces to Protect the Emperor, proposed that the Bakufu try its best to convince Choshu to retreat, and only resort to fighting if the rebels persisted.

Yoshinobu's views were accepted, and the court issued an Imperial edict stating that the Satsuma-Aizu coup of the previous summer was in complete harmony with the Emperor's will, and that the Choshu troops must withdraw and await further Imperial orders. When the edict reached the Choshu commanders at their camps, they flatly rejected it as "mere treachery by the Bakufu and Satsuma traitors" who surrounded the Emperor. The Bakufu then set July seventeenth as the deadline for the withdrawal of Choshu troops from Kyoto.

At dawn on July nineteenth, the first cannon shots thundered through the city. Choshu's second attack on the gates of the Imperial Palace would be the deathblow to the movement of *Imperial Reverence and Expelling the Barbarians*. The Battle at the Forbidden Gates, which had begun at dawn, ended in disaster for the Choshu Loyalists on the same afternoon. They were forced by their Aizu and Satsuma foes to retreat, and having been branded an "Imperial Enemy" for firing on the palace gates, the men of Choshu once again returned home in disgrace. Although the actual fighting ended in a matter of hours, Kyoto continued to burn for three days, as much of the city was consumed by flames.

While the British bombardment of Kagoshima had taught Satsuma the futility of fighting with Western powers, its enemies in Choshu continued its anti-foreign antics. This is not to say that Choshu still believed exclusion possible; rather, its intention was to humiliate the Bakufu, while displaying its unconditional dedication to the xenophobic Emperor, although he had banished that clan from Kyoto. After the first bombardment of Shimonoseki, Choshu had rebuilt its batteries, and constructed new ones, upon which it mounted all the guns it could accumulate.

In June, Great Britain, France, The Netherlands and the United States had informed Edo that unless their ships could be assured safe passage through Shimonoseki Strait they would bombard the Shimonoseki coast. Not only was Edo unable to control Choshu — which at that time had been planning the countercoup in Kyoto — but it secretly welcomed a bombardment. The Bakufu had even loaned maps of Japan to France, so that the foreigners could more easily punish the renegade clan. The Westerners' purpose for the joint-bombardment of Shimonoseki is summed up in the words of Ernest Satow, then-interpreter to the British minister in Japan: *"We had, it might be said, conquered the goodwill of Satsuma, and a similar process applied to the other principal head of the anti-foreign party might well be expected to produce an equally wholesome effect."*

On the afternoon of August fifth, the four-nation fleet, consisting of seventeen warships carrying a combined total of 288 cannon and over 5,000 troops, bombarded the Shimonoseki coast, destroying all the Choshu forts in a single day, before landing to easily overtake the six hundred samurai defending the coastline. On August fourteenth, a peace treaty was signed between Choshu and the four nations. Ironically, Choshu's unyielding xenophobic sentiment led to the downfall of the anti-foreign movement. The completion of the peace treaty silenced once and for all the cries to expel the foreigners for the sake of the Emperor, for by agreeing to its terms Choshu automatically abandoned its xenophobic policy, and its claim that it alone was the true champion of the Imperial Court. From this time forward Choshu would concentrate on one great purpose: toppling the Tokugawa Bakufu. To this end, the foreigners, namely Great Britain, would play a crucial role: thus Choshu's sudden change in attitude toward the Westerners, at the expense of the Tokugawa. *"Having beaten the Chôshiû people,"* Satow wrote, *"we had come to like and respect them, while a feeling of dislike began to arise in our minds for the Tycoon's* people on account of their weakness and double-dealing, and from this time onwards I sympathized more and more with the daimiô party,** from whom the Tycoon's government had always tried to keep us apart."*

Accordingly, by August 1864, Satsuma and Choshu, though bitter enemies, both enjoyed amicable relations with the British, relations which would prove invaluable in the turbulent years ahead. Through actual warfare with the West, these two leaders of the coming revolution finally realized the futility of trying to expel the foreigners by military force.

Eight days after the foreign bombardment of Shimonoseki, the

*Shogun's

**Choshu and Satsuma

Bakufu issued a decree to twenty-one feudal clans to prepare their armies for a military expedition against Choshu. Edo would use Choshu's recent misfortunes, including its present status as "Imperial Enemy," to regain absolute authority.

The attempt was futile. The Bakufu was gradually losing the upper hand it had recently recaptured. A lack of consensus between the government ministers in Edo and Lord Yoshinobu, Inspector General of the Forces Protecting the Emperor in Kyoto, delayed the expedition. Yoshinobu, whose long stay in Kyoto afforded him a better understanding of the situation there than that of his counterparts in Edo, took care not to disturb the delicate balance between the court and the various clans. The ministers in Edo distrusted Yoshinobu, whom they mistakenly suspected of scheming with the court to wrest control of the political power for himself. Furthermore, some of the *daimyo* who had been ordered to take part in the expedition had long sympathized with Choshu. Others preferred solving their own financial difficulties to waging a costly war, which, if successful, would only strengthen the Bakufu at the expense of their respective domains.

Although by mid-November the Bakufu had massed some 150,000 troops at the Choshu borders awaiting the command to attack, the expedition would not yet be launched. Since the failed countercoup in Kyoto the previous summer, followed by the bombardment of Shimonoseki, Choshu had split into two factions. The conservatives blamed the radicals for the great losses their clan had suffered, not the least of which was Choshu's having been branded an "Imperial Enemy." The conservatives favored "pledging allegiance to the Bakufu" at any cost in order to preserve themselves. The radicals, meanwhile, called for "military preparation to fight the Bakufu." However, with the death of the movement for *Imperial Reverence and Expelling the Barbarians,* the conservatives, for the time being, had gained the upper hand.

Meanwhile Satsuma had undergone a change of heart concerning their relationships with both Choshu and Edo. The leader of the Satsuma military, Saigo Kichinosuke, had been appointed staff officer of Edo's expeditionary forces against Choshu, putting him in command of the troops of twenty-three clans. But Saigo no longer thought it necessary to crush Choshu. Rather, he realized that the mere presence of this most radical of clans was a constant menace to the Tokugawa, serving to neutralize the authority of Satsuma's erstwhile ally. Using the internal discord in Choshu, Saigo was able to arrive at a compromise with the Choshu conservatives that the Bakufu accepted, and avoid a costly war for all concerned. At the risk of assassination, Saigo had personally gone to Shimonoseki to present Choshu with a set of conditions for avoiding war, the boldness of which earned him the respect of allies and foes alike. Among these conditions was a call for the Lord of Choshu to send a letter of apology to the Bakufu for his "criminal attack on the Imperial capital." In addition, the three Choshu officials responsible for the attack would be ordered to commit *seppuku,* and their staff commanders executed. The Lord of Choshu accepted Saigo's conditions, and war was avoided.

Tension continued to mount between the conservatives and rebels of Choshu, with the latter group emerging victorious in a civil war within that domain. Had the Choshu rebels been defeated, it is likely that their clan would have continued indefinitely under conservative rule. Instead, the Loyalists' resumption of power in February 1865 would prove to be a vital turning point in the struggle to overthrow the Bakufu.

Two months later, in April 1865, the Tokugawa ordered a second military expedition against the renegade domain. However, before the Bakufu would actually launch its ill-fated expedition in June 1866, a political outlaw from the Tosa clan would broker a military alliance between Satsuma and Choshu, and in so doing change the course of history. The Satsuma-Choshu Alliance, the first union between any of the clans since the establishment of the Tokugawa Bakufu, was realized on

January 21, 1866, the result of a yearlong struggle by Sakamoto Ryoma and his band of renegades. This alliance, which formed the most powerful military force in the nation, was the beginning of the end of the Tokugawa Bakufu.

Before the Bakufu would suffer a humiliating defeat at the hands of a single clan, it would be stunned by still another misfortune. In July 1866, Shogun Iemochi suddenly took ill and died at his stronghold of Osaka Castle, and the Shogunate found itself without a Shogun.

Iemochi's most logical heir was Lord Yoshinobu of Mito, whose campaign several years before to succeed then-Shogun Iesada had been crushed by Ii Naosuke. In August, exactly one week after Iemochi's death, Yoshinobu became the fifteenth Head of the House of Tokugawa. For thirteen generations acceptance of this position had been tantamount to succeeding the Shogun, an appointment which Tokugawa Yoshinobu now shrewdly declined. He was aware of his unpopularity, particularly among the Bakufu ministers at Edo; and so, despite repeated entreaties by several leading men of the Tokugawa camp, all of whom considered him the only man capable of saving the Bakufu, the twenty-nine-year-old Head of the House of Tokugawa remained adamant in his refusal, and still a fifteenth Shogun had not been named. Lord Yoshinobu was confident that the time would come when his enemies within the Bakufu would beg him to succeed to the post. Meanwhile, he attended to his military duties in the expedition against Choshu.

While Choshu had managed to arm itself with superior weaponry through the good offices of Satsuma and Sakamoto Ryoma's group, its forces numbered only four thousand, against the tens of thousands of pro-Tokugawa troops from thirty-one clans. But the fighters of Choshu, conscripted from among both peasants and samurai, fought with a moral conviction which the Tokugawa armies lacked. One Tokugawa commander, despairing of victory, had sent a letter to Edo Castle, pointing out that the enemy had the backing of Great Britain, and that it was determined to emerge victorious. Indeed, the entire Choshu domain was fighting for its very survival. The impending Bakufu attack had created a new sense of unity throughout Choshu, despite the recent civil war there. Choshu was now united in its determination to defend itself: should it be defeated, its *daimyo* would be punished, its samurai lose their stipends, the stores of its merchants looted, and the lands and crops of its peasants destroyed.

In contrast, the various *daimyo* who had supposedly sided with the Bakufu had been reluctant to deploy troops for lack of a clear reason to fight. This further diminished the already low morale of the Tokugawa troops, for whom Edo lacked sufficient supplies of food and gold. And although the Tokugawa Navy was clearly superior, the Choshu Army, equipped with rapid-firing, breech-loading rifles and cannon, was better armed than nearly all of the Bakufu's land forces, which had to resort to muskets, swords, spears and the ancient armor of their ancestors. "*The war has already been lost*," declared the Tokugawa commander, and shortly after the Bakufu forces were defeated along the second of four war fronts.

Although a Choshu victory was inevitable by August, hostilities were officially suspended in September as beneficial to both sides. In truth, however, the Bakufu was crumbling. Defeat at the hands of a single clan had not only demoralized its own samurai, but had also made it clear to the entire nation that the Tokugawa hegemony of over two and a half centuries had, for all means and purposes, ended. With the exception of the Tokugawa-related clans, the Bakufu had now lost the support of virtually all of the feudal domains in Japan.

Satsuma and the anti-Bakufu nobles in Kyoto now used the political vacuum created by Choshu's victory, the death of the Shogun, and the refusal of Yoshinobu to succeed him, to strengthen their position at court. Although Emperor Komei and his top advisors were staunch supporters of the Tokugawa, the anti-Bakufu faction at court, with the cooperation of Satsuma, was planning the restoration of Imperial rule. Why, one might ask, would the Emperor bitterly oppose those who would restore his divine line to the pinnacle of power in his sacred empire? The answer is simple: So great was his fear of anything Western, that he preferred the political authority remain in the hands of the Commander in Chief of the Expeditionary Forces Against the Barbarians, who, until recently, had kept the foreigners out and Japan at peace for centuries. Thus Emperor Komei's hate for Choshu and all other radical elements, who for the past several years had been plotting to shatter the state of things by destroying his sturdiest shield, the Tokugawa Bakufu.

The leader of the plot at court to overthrow the Bakufu and restore the Emperor to power was Lord Iwakura Tomomi, a previously high-ranking court noble, who was now operating in exile from the outskirts of Kyoto. Six years earlier, Lord Iwakura had urged the Emperor to sanction the marriage between the princess and the Shogun, as a means of uniting the court and the Bakufu. "Then," this master of political intrigue had explained to the Emperor, "if you would order the Bakufu to first consult with the court before making any decisions involving either domestic or foreign matters, Edo would maintain political authority in name only, with the actual power resting in the hands of the Imperial Court." His intentions mistaken as traitorous by the Loyalists in Kyoto, Lord Iwakura was banished by the court, partly for his own safety, in the summer of 1862, but was now once again actively plotting the overthrow of the Bakufu.

During his past four years in exile, Lord Iwakura had been in secret contact with several leaders of the revolution. At the end of August, after Edo's defeat to Choshu, Lord Iwakura had organized a group of twenty-two court nobles to deliver a memorial to the Emperor. The memorial called for the formation of a council of lords in Kyoto to decide the affairs of state, and a political reformation within the court. The suggestion was tantamount to the impeachment of the Emperor's leading advisors, all of whom supported Edo. The plan backfired, and at the end of October the Emperor ordered the detention of the twenty-two nobles who had submitted the memorial, and a tighter watch on Lord Iwakura's home in exile. At the beginning of December the anti-Bakufu radicals were struck with yet another blow: Yoshinobu yielded to pressure from the Imperial Court and his own ministers, and agreed to become the fifteenth Tokugawa Shogun in a final effort to save the Bakufu. Then less than three weeks later, on December twenty-fifth, Shogun Yoshinobu met with his worst disaster since the defeat of his armies to Choshu.

Emperor Komei suddenly died at age thirty-six, and although the official medical report attributed the cause of death to smallpox, rumor had it that the Son of Heaven had been poisoned. This was not a farfetched conclusion. Alive, Emperor Komei presented a serious obstacle to both Lord Iwakura and Satsuma in their mutual goal of toppling the Bakufu. What's more, the Imperial heir was only fourteen years old; his maternal grandfather and official guardian had for years been an opponent of Edo, and was in a perfect position to aid his longtime ally Lord Iwakura. To the revolutionaries in Choshu and Satsuma, to the renegades in Kyoto, and to the Bakufu elite in Edo and Osaka, the death of Emperor Komei marked the beginning of a new political age.

Lord Iwakura's ideas of a conciliar government had long been in the minds of prominent Loyalists, most of whom advocated annihilating the Tokugawa. In June 1867, as the Loyalists, led by Satsuma, Choshu and the Iwakura faction at court, were preparing to crush the Bakufu by military force, Sakamoto Ryoma devised a plan to avoid a bloody civil war. The plan, which was nothing less than a call for democracy in Japan, urged the Shogun to abdicate and restore power to the Imperial

Court. It advocated the establishment of two legislative houses of government — one upper, one lower — to be filled by men of ability among the feudal lords, court nobles, and representatives of the Japanese people at large. All government measures, the plan stated, should be decided by the councilors on the basis of public opinion. Ryoma's plan was endorsed by the influential Lord of Tosa, who submitted it to the Shogun in October 1867.

On October fourteenth the Shogun announced in the Grand Hall of Nijo Castle, the Tokugawa stronghold in Kyoto, his decision to abdicate and restore the Imperial Court to power. Ryoma's plan, as it happened, came at the eleventh hour. Support for the Bakufu among the clans was waning. A promise to Edo of military aid by the French had not been realized, while Britain supported Satsuma and Choshu. Had Yoshinobu waited much longer, he would have found his armies engaged in battle with the combined forces of Satsuma, Choshu and any number of other feudal lords who had previously sworn allegiance to the Tokugawa but were now compelled to fight under the Imperial banner. In fact, on the day after the Shogun's announcement, a secret Imperial decree bearing the Emperor's seal was issued to the representatives of Satsuma and Choshu, authorizing their armies, and those of all the *daimyo* who were "loyal" to the Emperor, to attack and destroy the Bakufu. Five days earlier, the Satsuma leaders had requested Lord Iwakura to draw up the decree. Iwakura immediately set to work on the document, which called for the destruction of the Bakufu, the punishment of the "traitor" Yoshinobu, and the deaths of the Lord of Aizu, who was the Bakufu's Protector of Kyoto, and his younger brother, the Lord of Kuwana, who was the Shogun's official representative in Kyoto in charge of inspecting the Imperial Court and its nobles. Iwakura entrusted the completed document to his confidant at court, the maternal grandfather and guardian of the fifteen-year-old Emperor. Early in the morning of the day after Yoshinobu had made the announcement, the Imperial decree, with the Emperor's seal secured by

Iwakura's confidant, was smuggled out of court and presented to the representatives of Satsuma and Choshu, while on the previous day, the Emperor had pardoned Choshu of all crimes.

The Aizu and Kuwana clans, supported by the Shinsengumi and other Tokugawa police units, were infuriated with Yoshinobu. Shortly after the Shogun's announcement they contemplated burning Satsuma's Kyoto estate, occupying the Imperial Palace, kidnapping the Emperor, and taking him to the Tokugawa fortress of Osaka Castle. Although the Shogun had indeed restored the power to the court, the oppositionist forces aptly likened the revolution to a game of chess, in that the side which controlled the Emperor controlled Japan.

Meanwhile, Yoshinobu vacillated between making good on his promise to abdicate or engaging the Imperial Forces in a bloody conflict. In a feeble attempt to avoid the inevitable, the Tokugawa camp launched a short-lived war against the Imperial Forces, just south of Kyoto in early January. His troops routed in just three days, Yoshinobu retreated from his Osaka stronghold to his fortress at Edo. The former Shogun did not vacate Edo Castle until February, five months after he had announced his abdication.

In March, Katsu Kaishu, as head of the Tokugawa Army, spared the city of Edo from the torch by personally surrendering the Shogun's castle to Saigo Kichinosuke, commander of the Imperial forces. Aizu continued to resist until September, when its castle fell to the Imperial Army. The war did not end until the last Tokugawa forces finally surrendered on the far-northern island of Ezo, in May 1869.

FAMILY CRESTS AND SYMBOLS

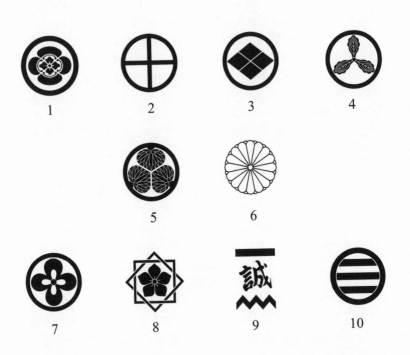

1 Katsu family crest
2 Shimazu family crest and symbol of Satsuma
3 Takasugi family crest
4 Yamanouchi family crest and symbol of Tosa
5 Tokugawa family crest and symbol of the Bakufu
6 Chrysanthemum crest and symbol of the Emperor
7 Takechi family crest
8 Sakamoto family crest
9 Symbol of the Shinsengumi
10 Kondo family crest

Aizu: A Tokugawa-related domain in northern Honshu.

Akamatsu Kosaburo: A celebrated military scientist.

Anenokoji Kintomo: A leader of radical court nobles.

Arima Tota: A Satsuma samurai and vice-chief of staff of the Imperial Army.

Asaemon: (see Yamada Asaemon)

Asakusa: A district in Edo.

Bakufu: (see Tokugawa Bakufu)

Chiba Dojo: A prestigious fencing school in Edo.

Chiba Sanako: Daughter of sword master of Chiba Dojo.

Choshu: A leading anti-Bakufu domain on the western end of Honshu.

daimyo: Lord of a feudal domain.

dojo: A martial arts training hall.

Edo: Bakufu capital.

Edogawa: A river which flows southward through the province of Shimo-usa, west of Edo, and through the western outskirts of Edo, emptying into Edo Bay.

Fushimi: A town near Kyoto.

Gion: A district in Kyoto.

Hamaguri Gate: One of Nine Forbidden Gates of the Imperial Palace in Kyoto.

Hayashi Kenzo: A Satsuma samurai.

Hijikata Toshizo: Vice-commander of the Shinsengumi.

Hikone: A pro-Tokugawa domain in western Honshu, ruled by Ii Naosuke.

Hirai Kao: A samurai woman of Tosa.

Hirai Shujiro: A Tosa samurai and lieutenant of Takechi Zuizan.

Hiroi Iwanosuke: A Tosa samurai.

Hirose Kenta: A Tosa samurai and lieutenant of Takechi Zuizan.

Hiroshima: A domain in southwestern Honshu, on the Inland Sea.

Hokushin-Itto Style: Style of fencing taught at Chiba Dojo, and studied by Sakamoto Ryoma.

Honma Seiichiro: A *ronin* from the province of Echigo.

Honshu: Largest of the four main Japanese islands.

Ii Naosuke (Lord Ii): Lord of Hikone and Bakufu regent.

Ikedaya: An inn in Kyoto.

Itabashi: A district in Edo.

Iwakura Tomomi (Lord Iwakura): Leader of anti-Bakufu faction at the Imperial Court.

Iyo: A province on Shikoku.

Izumi: A province northwest of Kii.

Kagamigawa: A river in Kochi Castletown.

Kagoshima: Castletown of Satsuma.

Kaientai (literally, "Naval Auxiliary Force"): A private navy and shipping firm established by Sakamoto Ryoma to run guns for the revolutionaries and to wage war against forces loyal to the Bakufu.

Kamogawa: A river in Kyoto.

Kanrin Maru: The first Japanese-manned ship to sail to the Western world.

Katsu Kaishu: Influential Bakufu naval commissioner.

Katsurahama: A beach in Kochi.

Kawaramachi: A district in Kyoto.

kenjutsu (literally, "sword techniques"): Japanese fencing.

Kii: A clan in central Honshu which was one of the Three Tokugawa Branch Houses and the native domain of Shogun Iemochi.

kimono: A gown worn by men and women.

Kobe: A fishing village and port on Osaka Bay which was the site of Katsu Kaishu's naval academy.

Kochi: Castletown of Tosa.

Kodenma-cho: A district in Edo and modern Tokyo, and location of Shogunate's official execution grounds.

Komei: A Japanese Emperor.

Kondo Isami: Commander of the Shinsengumi.

Kuwana: A pro-Bakufu domain in central Honshu.

Kyoto: Imperial capital.

Kyushu: One of four main Japanese islands, southwest of Honshu.

Masaki Tetsuma: A Tosa samurai and lieutenant of Takechi Zuizan.

Matsudaira (House of): Ruling family of Aizu clan and close Tokugawa relative.

Mibu: A district in Kyoto and location of Shinsengumi headquarters.

Mito: A domain just northeast of Edo which was one of the Three Tokugawa Branch Houses, and the birthplace of Tokugawa Yoshinobu and *Imperial Loyalism*.

Miura Kyutaro: A samurai and elite official of the Kii clan.

Musashi: A province southwest of Edo.

Mutsu Yonosuke: Sakamoto Ryoma's right-hand man and leader of the Executive Committee to avenge Ryoma's murder.

Nagare-yama: A village on the left bank of the Edogawa, in the province of Shimo-usa.

Nagasaki: An open port city under Bakufu control in western Kyushu, on the East China Sea.

Narahara Kizaemo: A Satsuma samurai.

Naharigawa: A river in Tosa.

Nakai Shogoro: A follower of Sakamoto Ryoma and member of the Executive Committee to avenge Ryoma's murder.

Nakamura Hanjiro (aka "The Butcher"): A notorious Satsuma swordsman and devoted follower of Saigo Kichinosuke.

Nakaoka Shintaro: A Tosa samurai and Sakamoto Ryoma's compatriot who was assassinated with him in Kyoto.

Namamugi: A village near Yokohama, and the scene of Richardson's murder.

Narahara Kizaemon: A Satsuma samurai.

Ohmiya: A soy dealer's shop in Kyoto which served as Ryoma's hideout.

Okada Izo: A Tosa samurai and assassin.

Osaka: Mercantile capital, located in western Honshu.

Otome: Sakamoto Ryoma's elder sister.

O-ume: Mistress of Serizawa Kamo.

ronin: A lordless- or outlaw-samurai.

ryo: A gold coin and unit of Japanese currency.

Saigo Kichinosuke (aka "Saigo the Great"): A Satsuma samurai and commander-in-chief of Imperial forces.

Sakamoto Gombei: Sakamoto Ryoma's elder brother.

Sakamoto Ryoma (aka Saitani Umetaro): A Tosa samurai who played a leading role in overthrowing the Bakufu.

sake: An alcoholic beverage fermented from rice.

samurai: A feudal warrior who served a *daimyo*.

-san: A polite suffix used after a person's name.

Satsuma: A leading anti-Bakufu domain in southern Kyushu.

Sawamura Sonojo: A Tosa samurai, follower of Sakamoto Ryoma and member of the Executive

Committee to avenge Ryoma's murder.

sensei: An honorary title used for people who possess special knowledge, including teachers and scholars. Used alone or as a suffix after a person's name.

seppuku (literally, "cutting the belly"): An honorable form of suicide practiced by samurai.

Serizawa Kamo: A commander of the Shinsengumi.

Shibamaki: A village in the mountains north of Kochi Castletown.

Shikoku: Smallest of the four main Japanese islands, located in southern Japan, east of Kyushu.

Shimabara: A licensed pleasure quarter of Kyoto.

Shimazu (House of): Ruling family of Satsuma.

Shimazu Hisamitsu (Lord Hisamitsu): Influential *de facto* Lord of Satsuma.

Shimazu Nariakira (Lord Nariakira): Lord of Satsuma who influenced Saigo Kichinosuke.

Shimoda: An open port southwest of Yokohama, and location of United States Consulate.

Shimonoseki: A port in Choshu on the western tip of Honshu.

Shimonoseki Strait: Strait between Honshu and Kyushu.

Shimo-usa: A province west of Edo.

Shinsengumi: A shogunal police corps in Kyoto.

Shogun: Commander in Chief of the Expeditionary Forces Against the Barbarians. Title of the Head of the House of Tokugawa and military ruler of feudal Japan.

Sumiya: A house in Kyoto's licensed pleasure quarter of Shimabara.

Susaki: A port in Tosa.

Tadahiro: Master swordsmith who produced the sword carried by Sakamoto Ryoma when he fled Tosa.

Takahashi Oden (aka "Evil Woman"): An attractive young murderess executed in Tokyo.

Takasegawa: A canal in Kyoto.

Takasugi Shinsaku: A radical leader of Choshu.

Takechi Hanpeita (aka Takechi Zuizan, Master Zuizan): Leader of Tosa Loyalist Party.

Takeda Kanryusai: A squad leader of the Shinsengumi.

Tanahashi Saburo (aka Matsube): Murderer of Hiroi Iwanosuke's father.

Tanaka Ryosuke: A friend of Sakamoto Ryoma.

Tanaka Shimbe: A Satsuma samurai and assassin.

tatami: Thickly woven straw mats, perfectly fitted together and covering the floor in traditional Japanese rooms.

Tauchi Tomo: A rank-and-file member of the Shinsengumi.

Tenmanya: An inn in Kyoto.

Tokaido: A road connecting Kyoto and Edo

Tokichi: Sakamoto Ryoma's manservant and bodyguard.

Tokugawa (House of): Ruling family of feudal Japan.

Tokugawa Bakufu: Tokugawa Shogunate. Military feudal government at Edo which dominated the Japanese nation.

Tokugawa Iemochi: Child-lord of Kii and the fourteenth Tokugawa Shogun.

Tokugawa Iesada: Thirteenth Tokugawa Shogun.

Tokugawa Ieyasu: Founder of the Tokugawa Bakufu and the first Tokugawa Shogun.

Tokugawa Yoshimune: Eighth Tokugawa Shogun.

Tokugawa Yoshinobu (aka Lord Yoshinobu): Fifteenth and last Tokugawa Shogun.

Tosa: A domain on the Pacific coast of southern Shikoku.

Yamada Asaemon VII (aka "The Beheader"): Unofficial executioner to the Shogunate, and designated sword-tester to the Shogun.

Yamada Asaemon VIII (aka Yoshifusa): Official executioner in Tokyo.

Yamanouchi Yodo (Lord Yodo): Influential Lord of Tosa.

Tamaki Yasuda, Mrs.: A friend of Sakamoto Ryoma's family.

Yodogawa: A river in Osaka.

Yokohama: A port town on Edo Bay just west of Edo, and location of foreign settlement.

Yoshida Toyo: Tosa regent assassinated by Loyalists in Kochi.

INDEX

INDEX

Hillsborough,
    Romulus.

Samurai sketches.

$29.95

5/24/01

DATE		